Palgrave Business Briefings

The *Business Briefings series* consists of short and authoritative introductory textbooks in core business topics. Written by leading academics, they take a no-nonsense, practical approach and provide students with a clear and succinct overview of the subject.

These textbooks put the needs of students first, presenting the topics in a meaningful way that will help students to gain an understanding of the subject area. Covering the basics and providing springboards to further study, these books are ideal as accessible introductions or as revision guides.

Other books in the Business Briefings series:

Research Methods, by Peter Stokes & Tony Wall

Marketing, by Jonathan Groucutt & Cheryl Hopkins

Organisational Behaviour, by Mike Maughan

Human Resource Management, by Michael Nieto

Quantitative Methods, by Les Oakshott

Financial Accounting, by Jill Collis

The Business Briefings Series
Series Standing Order ISBN 978–0–230–36385–4

You can receive future titles in this series as they are published by placing a standing order. Please contact your bookseller or, in the case of difficulty, write to us at the address below with your name and address, the title of the series and the ISBN quoted above.

Customer Services Department, Macmillan Distribution Ltd, Houndmills, Basingstoke, Hampshire, RG21 6XS, UK

MANAGEMENT ACCOUNTING

JILL COLLIS

First published 2016 by
PALGRAVE

Palgrave in the UK is an imprint of Macmillan Publishers Limited, registered in England, company number 785998, of 4 Crinan Street, London, N1 9XW.

Palgrave Macmillan in the US is a division of St Martin's Press LLC, 175 Fifth Avenue, New York, NY 10010.

Palgrave is a global imprint of the above companies and is represented throughout the world.

Palgrave® and Macmillan® are registered trademarks in the United States, the United Kingdom, Europe and other countries.

ISBN 978–1–137–33589–0 paperback

This book is printed on paper suitable for recycling and made from fully managed and sustained forest sources. Logging, pulping and manufacturing processes are expected to conform to the environmental regulations of the country of origin.

A catalogue record for this book is available from the British Library.

A catalog record for this book is available from the Library of Congress.

Printed in China

CONTENTS

LIST OF FIGURES

LIST OF TABLES

PREFACE TO MANAGEMENT ACCOUNTING

With tuition fees at a high level, many students find the purchase of a traditional text book is something that they have to compromise on, and either rely on the lecturer's handouts or borrow books from the library or friends. Unfortunately, this approach is rarely successful as it can only provide a partial and superficial understanding of the subject. This is particularly true of accounting, which many students find difficult.

The book is part of Palgrave's 'Business Briefings' series. It is designed to be succinct, but cover the basics of the subject. This means it is likely to be much more affordable. Students will still need to consult other texts to widen their knowledge of the subject, but this book offers a good introduction and can easily be used for revision purposes.

Most accounting courses taught in universities and colleges follow a syllabus that reflects the professional exams taken by accountants. This book covers the main topics associated with management accounting in a logical sequence. It starts by explaining the accountancy profession, the nature and purpose of accounting, and setting the business context. It then moves on to explain why managers in the manufacturing sector need to know the total cost of each product and shows how a total cost statement provides data for calculating the selling price. The next two chapters describe the methods used to identify the costs that can be traced directly to the product, and how absorption costing is used to apportion the indirect costs. The reader is then introduced to an alternative costing method for indirect costs known as activity-based costing, which can also be used to cost products or services. The final costing technique covered is marginal costing which is used for short-term decisions in businesses where the sales or production levels of products tend to fluctuate. The focus then moves to the important subject of budgetary control and the associated technique known as standard costing.

Each chapter has the same structure:

Objectives	Key points
Introduction	Revision questions
Main content	

The main content of each chapter explains the basics of the topic and case studies are used as examples or to show how the techniques are applied.

The key points section is a useful summary of the chapter and will be invaluable as part of a revision strategy. The revision questions are based on the material covered in the chapter and should allow the reader to gauge his or her understanding of the technique covered. Solutions to these questions can be found at the end of the book as well as on the companion website. www.palgrave.com/companion/Collis-Management-Accounting.

ACKNOWLEDGEMENTS

The author is grateful to Roger Hussey and Andrew Holt for permission to adapt some of their material for use in this book.

1

INTRODUCTION TO MANAGEMENT ACCOUNTING

1.1 OBJECTIVES

This chapter provides an introduction to accounting in a business context, and management accounting in particular. After studying this chapter, you should be able to:
- Identify the main professional accountancy bodies.
- Explain the need for a code of ethics for professional accountants.
- Explain the nature and purpose of accounting.
- Distinguish between financial accounting and management accounting.
- Compare different types of business entity.

1.2 THE ACCOUNTANCY PROFESSION

A professional accountant in the UK or the Republic of Ireland must pass a number of rigorous examinations set by one of the recognised accountancy bodies and pay an annual subscription to become a member of that body. The examinations cover a wide range of topics such as business and finance, financial and management accounting, financial reporting, auditing, taxation, law, business strategy and financial management. Table 1.1 shows the worldwide membership of the six chartered accountancy bodies, plus one other body that offers a recognised audit qualification, at 31 December 2014.

Once qualified, accountants can set up in practice on their own or with partners, or seek employment in an existing accountancy practice. Others may choose to work as accountants in industry and commerce, or in the public or voluntary sectors. Some accountants qualify with a view to working in the family business and those with entrepreneurial ideas may choose to start a new enterprise.

Large businesses are likely to have sufficient resources to employ a number of accounting and finance specialists, whereas medium-sized entities may employ one

Table 1.1 Worldwide membership of UK and Irish accountancy bodies

	Number	%
Association of Chartered Certified Accountants (ACCA)	174,227	36
Institute of Chartered Accountants in England and Wales (ICAEW)	144,167	30
Chartered Institute of Management Accountants (CIMA)	99,942	20
Chartered Accountants Ireland (CAI)	23,778	5
Institute of Chartered Accountants in Scotland (ICAS)	20,401	4
Chartered Institute of Public Finance and Accountancy (CIPFA)	13,327	3
Association of International Accountants	9,250	2
Total	485,092	100

Source: FRC, 2015, p. 11

accountant who is responsible for financial and management accounting functions, supported by other staff, such as a credit controller and bookkeeper. Very small entities often find it more cost effective to use an external accountant.

Professional accountants have a duty to serve the public interest because they are involved in the preparation and auditing of published financial information. Accountants and auditors are guided in their work by a code of ethics. *Ethics* are moral principles that underpin what is considered right and wrong in society, and how people should behave (Waite, 2012).

> **Activity**
> How ethical are you? Imagine you came out of a restaurant and found that the waiter had not charged you for your dessert. Would you go back and tell him?

You have to ask yourself whether you are happy to tell everyone (not just your friends, but your family and your teachers or boss) and how you would defend your actions if you were challenged. An ethical person would go back and tell the waiter or the manager, so the correct answer is 'Yes'. The important thing to realise is that ethics are not always about what other people might do, but about honesty and personal integrity.

The need for high values and consistent, ethical behaviour across the accountancy profession led to the development of an international code of ethics by the International Ethics Standards Board of Accountants (IESBA). The *Code of Ethics* for *Professional Accountants* (the IESBA Code) is published by the *International Federation of Accountants (IFAC)*, which is an association of professional bodies of accountants throughout the world. IFAC was founded in 1977 and in 2014 had 172 members and associates in 129 countries and jurisdictions, representing approximately 2.5 million accountants (including those in Table 1.1).

The IESBA Code requires a professional accountant to comply with five fundamental principles (IESBA, 2013, para 100.5):

(a) Integrity – to be straightforward and honest in all professional and business relationships.

(b) Objectivity – to not allow bias, conflict of interest or undue influence of others to override professional judgments.

(c) Professional Competence and Due Care – to maintain professional knowledge and skill at the level required to ensure that a client or employer receives competent professional services based on current developments in practice, legislation and techniques and act diligently and in accordance with applicable technical and professional standards.

(d) Confidentiality – to respect the confidentiality of information acquired as a result of professional and business relationships, and, therefore, not disclose any such information to third parties without proper and specific authority, unless there is a legal or professional right or duty to disclose, nor use the information for the personal advantage of the professional accountant or third parties.

(e) Professional Behavior – to comply with relevant laws and regulations and to avoid any action that discredits the profession.

Activity

Jane Goodfellow is an accountant at Vinyl Products Ltd. She recently noticed that the price of one of the materials used in the production process had gone up significantly, and this coincided with a change of supplier. When she tried asking the purchasing manager, Simon Buckfast, about it, he more or less told her to mind her own business, adding, "I've known the managing director of this new supplier for years and, in any case, it's my job to decide which suppliers we use!" Around this time, Jane also noticed that Simon had started driving an expensive new car to work. She suspects that the two events are connected, which might indicate fraud. Should she (a) turn a blind eye, (b) challenge Simon further, or (c) discuss the matter with another senior manager?

The facts are that the cost of materials has risen as a result of changing the supplier and Simon is responsible for the decision. Jane has an ethical dilemma because she is concerned about Simon's dismissive response, weak justification for the change in supplier, and luxurious new car. She suspects fraud and wonders what the best action would be. To ensure that she behaves with integrity, objectivity and professional competence, she should take action (b) followed by (c) if necessary.

1.3   NATURE AND PURPOSE OF ACCOUNTING

In its broadest form, accounting is a service provided to those who need financial information. In everyday language, *accounting* for something means giving an explanation or report on something. The following definition is taken from the *Oxford Dictionary of Accounting*.

> **Definition**
> Accounting is the process of identifying, measuring, recording and communicating economic transactions.
>
> Source: Law, 2010, p. 6

This book is concerned with the role of accounting in the private sector rather than public or voluntary contexts, so *economic transactions* refer to the money-making activities of the business that are concerned with creating wealth for the owner(s). We will now examine each stage in the accounting process:

- Identifying economic transactions is fairly straightforward in most cases. Examples include selling goods and services to customers, paying employees, purchasing inventories (goods for resale) and buying equipment (for use in the business) from suppliers. It is also important to distinguish between the economic transactions of the business and the personal economic transactions of the owner(s) and manager(s). Thus, the first stage in the accounting process leads to the classification of the economic transactions of the business into categories, such as purchase, sales revenue and salaries.
- Measuring economic transactions in monetary terms is convenient. It also makes it easier to aggregate, summarise and compare transactions.
- Recording economic transactions is essential. Traditionally transactions were recorded in handwritten books of accounts known as ledgers, but today most businesses record transactions in a computerised accounting system. Small businesses may use spreadsheets or a simple accounting software package, but larger

businesses with a wider range and volume of transactions use sophisticated software that may form part of an enterprise resource planning system.
• Communicating economic transactions is achieved by generating a variety of financial statements from the records in the accounting system. These are presented in a format that summarises a particular financial aspect of the business.

Activity

A business buys 5 litres of paint and 20 metres of timber and employs a carpenter for two days to build shelves in an office. Paint costs £4 per litre, timber costs £2.50 per metre and the carpenter charges £50 per day. What is the total cost of the shelves?

The cost can be calculated in a number of stages. You need to multiply the cost of paint per litre by the amount used. You also need to multiply the cost of timber per metre by the amount used. Finally, you need to calculate the cost of employing the carpenter by multiplying his daily rate by the number of days. The order in which you work out the figures does not matter, as long as you arrive at three figures which, when added together, make up the total cost of the job:

	£
Cost of paint (£4 × 5 litres)	20
Cost of timber (£2.50 × 20 metres)	50
Cost of labour (£50 × 2 days)	100
Total cost of the shelves	170

In more complex examples it is not so easy to identify and measure the economic events in monetary terms. We will be looking at some of these problems in subsequent chapters.

The *purpose of accounting* in the private sector is to provide financial information that helps the business achieve its objectives. This might be to maximise profits or to make sufficient profit to maintain the lifestyle desired by the owner(s).

1.4   OVERVIEW OF MANAGEMENT ACCOUNTING

Accounting can be divided into two main branches: management accounting and financial accounting. The purpose of *management accounting* is to provide managers with financial and other quantitative information to help them carry out their responsibilities for planning, controlling and decision making. The emphasis is on providing information to internal users that will help the business achieve its financial objectives. On the other hand, the purpose of *financial accounting* is to provide financial information to meet the needs of external users (those not involved in managing the business). Unlike management accounting, financial accounting is governed by regulations.

> **Definition**
> Management accounting is the branch of accounting concerned with collecting and analyzing financial and other quantitative information. It is primarily concerned with communicating information to management to help effective performance measurement, planning, controlling and decision making.
>
> Source: Collis, Holt and Hussey, 2012, p. 18

Performance measurement involves developing financial and non-financial indicators of progress towards the organisation's goals and regularly reviewing progress. Non-financial measures might include delivery time, customer retention and staff turnover. *Planning* includes developing budgets for future activities and operations and *controlling* involves using techniques for highlighting any adverse variances between the budgeted and actual figures to ensure that revenue targets are achieved and costs are within acceptable levels.

Management accounting can be divided into the following main activities:

- *Cost accounting* focuses on techniques for recording costs that help managers ascertain the cost of cost units, such as products and services, and cost centres. This allows management to make important decisions, such as setting selling prices and production/sales targets, and deciding which products or services are the most profitable to produce/sell. Another important aspect of cost accounting is establishing budgets and standard costs, and comparing them with the actual costs incurred. Large organisations may employ a cost accountant; smaller businesses may use the services of an external accountant. Cost accounting provides the cost and expenditure figures that are needed by the financial accountant when the business prepares its annual financial statements.
- *Managerial accounting* focuses on the processing and reporting components of management accounting.

Management accounting is widely used and is not confined to large firms. Research shows that a large majority of owner-managers of small companies use monthly or quarterly management accounts and budgets in addition to cash flow information and bank statements to help them manage the business (Collis and Jarvis, 2002).

Although accounting can be divided into financial and management accounting, you should not be misled into thinking that there is no relationship between these two activities, simply because they both draw on the same data sources. However, there are some important differences, which relate to the level of detail and timing of the information produced. Financial accounting operates on the basis of an annual reporting cycle and the preparation of the financial statements of limited liability entities is highly regulated to ensure that external users receive high quality, reliable information. However, the annual report and accounts is not published until some months after the end of the financial year. By contrast, management accounting is not regulated at all, which means the information can be provided to internal users in the form they want it and as often as they want it. In both large and small businesses, detailed management accounting information for each activity in each part of the business is produced on a weekly, monthly or quarterly basis. If the periodic management accounts for the different parts of a business were aggregated, the totals would be very similar to the figures in the financial accounts, although there would be some differences. For example, the financial accounts would contain information on finance costs (such as interest paid on loans) and taxation, whereas the management accounts are likely to contain more estimated figures.

1.5   TYPES OF BUSINESS ENTITY

In the UK the legal form of businesses in the *private sector* can be classified into three main types:

- Sole proprietorships.
- Partnerships.
- Companies (and other incorporated entities).

At the start of 2014, the number of private sector enterprises in the UK stood at a record 5.2 million. Figure 1.1 shows how they were dispersed among the three main categories.

The size of private sector enterprises ranges from very small businesses, such as sole proprietorships and one person companies with no employees, to large international companies with thousands of owners and employees. Of the total of 5.2 million businesses in the UK, 99.9% were small (fewer than 50 employees) or medium-sized (fewer than 250 employees) (BIS, 2014b, p. 1). In addition to providing a living for their owners, these small and medium-sized entities (SMEs) contributed to the economy by providing 60% of employment and 47% of turnover in the private sector.

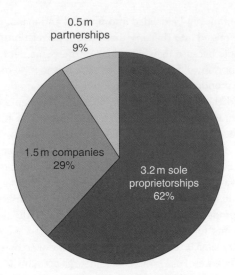

Figure 1.1 UK private sector enterprises by legal status
Source: BIS, 2014a, Table 3

The majority of smaller entities are owner-managed and family-owned (SBS, 2004; Collis, 2008). In larger businesses, it is more likely that ownership and control will become separated, and the owners will appoint managers to run the business on their behalf. Businesses also differ in terms of their legal status and in the groups of people who are likely to be interested in financial information about them.

To a large extent, the range of users of the financial information depends on the size of the business. For example, financial information relating to a small shop is likely to be used only by the owner-manager and the tax authorities, whereas financial information relating to a large international company will be of interest not only to managers within the business but also to investors, lenders, suppliers, customers and other external parties, such as competitors. Each user group needs financial information for a different purpose. A manager working in a division of a large company is likely to require detailed information in order to run the department, a bank lending officer contemplating lending £1 million to a business is likely to need information for assessing the lending risk, and a supplier will need information for assessing the risk of supplying goods and/or services on credit to the business.

Accounting provides important financial information that helps businesses achieve their economic objectives. Some business owners want to increase their wealth by maximising profit while others simply want to make sufficient profit to maintain a certain lifestyle.

Sole proprietorships

The majority of businesses are *sole proprietorships*. A sole proprietorship is an unincorporated entity owned by one person, who is in business with a view to making a profit. The business may be providing a service (for example, a window cleaner, hairdresser or business consultant), trading goods (for example a newsagent, florist or grocer) or making goods (for example, a cabinet maker, potter or dress designer). Alternatively, it may have activities in the primary sector (agriculture, forestry or fishing). The owner may run the business alone or employ staff.

The owner of a sole proprietorship has *unlimited liability*, which means that he or she is personally liable for any debts the business may incur. This liability extends beyond any original investment and could mean the loss of personal assets. There are no legal formalities to set up this type of business, but an entrepreneur wanting to start a sole proprietorship may experience difficulty in obtaining finance, as the capital is restricted to what he or she has available to invest, supplemented by what he or she can borrow. The owner must keep accounting records, but there is no obligation to disclose financial information to the public.

Partnerships

There are two types of *partnership*: unincorporated partnerships and limited liability partnerships (LLPs). An *unincorporated partnership* is an entity in which two or more people join together in business with a view to making a profit. Unincorporated partnerships are a popular form of business for professional firms such as accountants, doctors, dentists and solicitors. The partners may run the business alone or employ staff.

The owners of an unincorporated partnership (the partners) have joint and several liability, which means they have unlimited liability for each other's acts in terms of any debts the business may incur. This liability extends beyond any original investment and could mean the loss of personal assets. The capital is restricted to what the partners have to invest, supplemented by what they can borrow. The *Business Names Act 1985* requires the names of the partners to be shown on business stationery, but they need not be used in the business name. The partners must keep accounting records, but there is no obligation to disclose financial information to the public.

The relationship between partners should be formalised in a partnership agreement. In the absence of a partnership agreement, or if the agreement does not cover a point in dispute, the *Partnership Act 1890* provides the following rules:

- Partners share equally in the profits or losses of the partnership
- Partners are not entitled to receive salaries
- Partners are not entitled to interest on their capital

- Partners may receive interest at 5% per annum on any advances over and above their agreed capital
- A new partner may not be introduced unless all the existing partners consent
- A retiring partner is entitled to receive interest at 5% per annum on his or her share of the partnership assets retained in the partnership after his or her retirement
- On dissolution of the partnership, the assets of the firm must be used first to repay outside creditors, second to repay partners' advances, and third to repay partners' capital. Any residue on dissolution should be distributed to the partners in the profit-sharing ratio (equally unless specified otherwise in the partnership agreement).

You may think that the partners do not need an agreement, because the Partnership Act 1890 sets out the relationship in case of dispute. However, relying on the Act means the rules of a standard agreement are applied, which may not be appropriate to the circumstances.

Activity

Indicate which of these characteristics apply to the following types of business:

		Sole proprietorship	Partnership
(a)	The entity is an unincorporated business	❑	❑
(b)	There is no maximum number of owners	❑	❑
(c)	There are no formalities involved when starting the business	❑	❑
(d)	There should be a contract of agreement	❑	❑
(e)	Accounting records must be kept	❑	❑

What sole proprietorships and unincorporated partnerships have in common is their unincorporated status, which means the owners have unlimited liability for any debts or losses incurred by the business. Of course, there is only one owner of a sole proprietorship, who is solely responsible, whereas the responsibility is shared in a partnership. A partnership can also raise more capital than a sole proprietorship because there are at least two owners (there is no maximum number of partners). For the same reason, a greater range of skills is likely to be available in a partnership. There are no formalities involved in setting up a sole proprietorship, but the relationship between partners should be formalised in a partnership agreement. All businesses, regardless of legal status must keep accounting records.

A *limited liability partnership (LLP)* is a partnership that through the process of incorporation acquires a legal status that is separate from that of its owners. An important advantage of an LLP is that each partner's liability for the debts and losses incurred by the business is limited to the amount of his or her investment in the business. There are two main exceptions to this limited liability:

- If a partner of an LLP is personally at fault, he or she may have unlimited liability if he or she accepted a personal duty of care or a personal contractual obligation.
- If an LLP becomes insolvent, the partners can be required to repay any property withdrawn from the LLP (including profits and interest) in the two years prior to insolvency. This applies where the partner could not reasonably have concluded that insolvency was likely.

LLPs are allowed to organise themselves internally in the same way as an unincorporated partnership, but the regulations that apply to them are similar to the requirements for companies. If one of the partners dies, his or her shares can be transferred to someone else and the business continues. On the other hand, when a partner in an unincorporated partnership dies, the partnership ceases. If the remaining partners want the business to continue, they need to form a new partnership, with or without additional partners.

Limited companies

The majority of limited liability entities are *limited companies*. A limited company is a business that through the process of incorporation acquires a legal status that is separate from that of its owners. The most common form of incorporation in the UK is through registration under the Companies Act 2006 (CA2006). The capital invested in the business is raised by selling shares to investors (hence the term *shareholder*), who are known as members. The capital invested in any type of business can be supplemented by loans and other forms of finance, such as trade credit from suppliers. Trade credit does not provide additional cash, but allows money already in the business to be used for other purposes until it is needed to pay creditors.

CA2006 defines a company as a limited company if the liability of its members is limited by its constitution. The company may be limited by shares or by guarantee. It is limited by shares if the members' liability is limited to the amount (if any) unpaid on the shares held by them. It is limited by guarantee if the members' liability is limited to such amount as they undertake to contribute to the assets of the company in the event of it being wound up.

> **Definition**
> Limited liability refers to the extent to which members of a limited company or LLP are liable for payment of the debts of the business.

Limited companies can be divided into *private companies* and *public companies*. More than 99% are private companies. A private company is any company that is not a public company. A public company is a company limited by shares or limited by guarantee and having share capital. Most companies are started as private limited companies. If a company grows sufficiently large, its owners may decide to convert it into a public company under the re-registration procedure in CA2006, which allows them to obtain a listing on a stock exchange and raise large amounts of capital. There are around 2,600 companies listed on the London Stock Exchange. Listed companies are important because they make a substantial contribution to the economy. Table 1.2 compares the main characteristics of public and private companies in the UK.

Figure 1.2 summarises the different types of business entity we have described.

Table 1.2 Main features of public and private companies

Public company	Private company
Must state in its memorandum of association that it is a public company	Defined as a company that is not a public company
Name must end with 'Public Limited Company' or 'PLC'	Name must end with 'Limited' or 'Ltd' or the Welsh equivalent
Can offer shares for sale on a stock exchange	Shares can be only be offered for sale privately
Must have at least one natural person not under 16 years of age as a director	Does not apply
Must have a company secretary (person or corporate) and hold an annual general meeting with members to pass resolutions	Does not apply
Must keep accounting records and publish financial statements complying with the Companies Act and accounting standards	Must keep accounting records and publish financial statements complying with the Companies Act and accounting standards
Must publish an annual report and accounts within 6 months of accounting year end	Must publish an annual report and accounts within 9 months of accounting year end
Extensive financial disclosure	Extent of financial disclosure depends on size and public interest

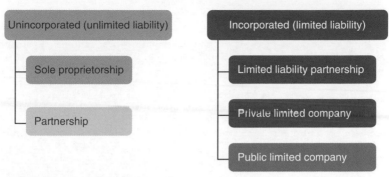

Figure 1.2 Types of business entity

1.6 KEY POINTS

A professional accountant in the UK must pass a number of rigorous examinations set by one of the recognised accountancy bodies and pay an annual subscription to become a member of that body. Accounting can be divided into two main branches. Financial accounting focuses on providing financial information to be communicated to external users. Management accounting focuses on providing financial information to internal users. It is used by managers for planning, controlling and decision making to help the business achieve its financial objectives.

There are a number of different legal forms of business in the UK. An unincorporated enterprise can be a sole proprietorship or a partnership; an incorporated business can take the form of a limited liability partnership or a limited liability company. A limited liability company can be registered as a private company or a public company. The legal form of the business has financial implications in terms of ability to raise capital, disclosure of financial information and the owners' responsibility for the debts incurred by the business.

REVISION QUESTIONS

1. Describe how a student can become a qualified professional accountant and explain the need for a code of ethics for professional accountants.
2. Describe the key elements of the definition of accounting.
3. Compare and contrast the two main branches of accounting.
4. Explain the advantages and disadvantages of a setting up a one-person business as a private limited company rather than a sole proprietorship.
5. Discuss the main differences between a public limited company and a private limited company in the UK, paying particular attention to the financial implications.

2
NEED FOR COST INFORMATION

2.1 OBJECTIVES

This chapter provides an introduction to cost accounting. It explains how detailed cost information can be used to ascertain the total cost of manufacturing a product and establishing its selling price. After studying this chapter, you should be able to:
- Explain why managers need to know the cost of producing products.
- Distinguish between direct costs and indirect costs.
- Distinguish between variable costs and fixed costs.
- Prepare a simple statement to calculate the total cost per unit.
- Calculate the selling price based on the total cost per unit.

2.2 IMPORTANCE OF COST INFORMATION

The need for a formal system that provides cost accounting information for management develops on a contingency basis. In a small business, the owner-manager may rely on tacit knowledge and informal methods, but this is not practical when the business grows larger and its activities become more complex. Table 2.1 summarises the key characteristics of small firms and compares them with those of their larger counterparts, where it is likely that the need for more detailed and timely information will lead to the development of formal systems of control.

In order to run a business successfully, those responsible for management need to know the *cost* of running the business. These costs include:

- The cost of goods sold in a trading business, the cost of goods produced in a manufacturing business, and the cost of any services provided by a business.
- The overhead expenses and other expenditure incurred in running the business.

There are a number of different ways of defining cost, but we will start with a general definition.

> **Definition**
> Cost is the expenditure on goods and services required to carry out the operations of an organization.
>
> Source: Law, 2010, p. 115

In a trading business, the cost of sales is calculated as:

Opening inventory + Purchases – Closing inventory

In a trading business, *inventory* refers to unsold goods the business has purchased with a view to selling them. However, in a manufacturing business, inventory refers to raw materials, work-in-progress and finished goods. In such a business, opening inventory is the value of the inventories of these three categories at the start of the accounting period. *Purchases* is the term for the raw materials and/or components purchased during the accounting period, and closing inventory refers to the value of inventories of raw materials, work-in-progress and finished goods at the end of the accounting period.

Guided by accounting principles, the accountant values opening inventory and purchases at the historical cost (the original cost paid for the items) and prudently values closing inventory at the lower of cost or net realisable value (selling price less costs of selling). Calculating the cost of goods sold for a trading business is relatively straightforward, but it is more complex for a business in the manufacturing industry or the service sector. It is even more difficult if more than one type of product or service is produced, because the cost of each product or service must be built up from the individual elements of cost that can be identified.

Table 2.1 Typical characteristics of small and large firms

Small firms	Large firms
Typically 1–2 owners	Many owners
Likely to be owner-managed	Managed by managers/directors
Little delegation of control	Control is delegated
Operations are relatively simple	Operations are complex and divided into functional areas
Multitasking is common	Need for functional specialists
Systems tend to be informal	Systems tend to be formal
Reliance on tacit knowledge	Reliance on explicit information

Business is about making money and managers are responsible for ensuring that the business meets its financial objectives. The main reasons why managers need cost information are:

- *To value inventory* – In a manufacturing business, managers need cost information to help them value inventories of raw materials, work-in-progress and unsold finished goods.
- *To plan production* – It would be very difficult to determine the best way to plan production without knowing the cost of producing the goods. It is necessary to know the cost of all the elements making up the production process and the funds required to support them. Such costs are not confined to materials and labour, but also include machinery, buildings, transport, administration, maintenance and many other items.
- *To maintain control* – Managers have no control if they do not know the costs incurred and are unable to compare them with the budgeted cost in their original plan. This could lead to the resources being employed inefficiently, resulting in waste and could lead to business failure.
- *To aid decision making* – It is essential for managers to have information about costs if they are to make the correct decisions. For example, they need cost information to decide whether to invest in new manufacturing machinery, to evaluate alternative ways of carrying out activities and to determine the selling prices of products and services.

A branch of management accounting, known as *cost accounting*, has developed to meet management's need for information about costs. This allows management to make important decisions which include setting the selling prices of its products and services, deciding which products and services are the most profitable, and setting its production and sales targets.

> **Definition**
> Cost accounting refers to the techniques used in collecting, processing and presenting financial and quantitative data within an organization to ascertain the cost of the cost centres, cost units and the various operations.
>
> Source: Law, 2010, p. 115

2.3   COST CENTRES AND COST UNITS

A *cost centre* is an identifiable part of the organisation for which costs can be collected such as an area of the business, function, activity or item of equipment.

Activity

Indicate which of the following could be cost centres in the following two businesses:

Toy manufacturer	Hotel
Assembly department	Kitchen
Stores department	Cost of drinks sold
Sales team	Reception area
Specialised moulding machine	Laundry
Salaries	Restaurant

You may not know anything about the manufacture of toys, but the definition of a cost centre given above should have helped you to identify the first four of these as possible cost centres. Salaries are usually an expense, not a cost centre. The specialised moulding machine may be a cost centre if it is sufficiently important and complex to allow a number of costs to be identified with that particular activity. Of course, not all toy manufacturers would use the same cost centres, but they are all areas of activity for which managers are likely to want to collect the costs. As far as the hotel is concerned, the cost of drinks sold is an expense, but all the others are potential cost centres.

Definition

A cost centre is the area of an organization for which costs are collected for the purpose of cost ascertainment, planning, decision making, and control.

Source: Law, 2010, p. 116

Cost centres are of two main types: *production cost centres* are those concerned with making a product, and *service cost centres* are those that provide services to different parts of the organisation. Identifying cost centres is relatively easy as they are usually clearly defined. One example is that of a factory canteen or a college refectory. In a manufacturing business, departments may be referred to as shops or workshops (for example, the machine shop). The sort of financial information that would be available for a canteen include employees' wages, the cost of electricity used for cooking, lighting and heating, the cost of food and beverages, etc.

A *cost unit* is a quantitative unit of the product or service to which costs are allocated. A cost unit can be:

- The final product (for example, a chair or a table in a furniture factory).
- A sub-assembly of a more complex product (for example, a car chassis in the motor industry).
- A batch of products where the unit cost of an individual product is very small (for example, a brick manufacturer may have a cost unit of 1,000 bricks, because the cost of one brick is so small that it would be difficult to measure).

In a manufacturing business it is fairly easy to identify the cost units, but it may be harder to identify the cost units for a business in the service sector. In a hotel or a nursing home the cost unit might be the room occupancy; in a logistics business the cost unit might be 1 tonne/mile (the cost involved in moving 1 tonne of goods over 1 mile); in a canteen, the number of meals served.

> ### Activity
> Suggest appropriate cost units for the following businesses:
>
> (a) A car manufacturer   (d) A sports centre
> (b) A carrier bag manufacturer   (e) A hairdresser
> (c) A plumber   (f) A dating agency

You may have identified some of the following cost units:

- A car manufacturer could use each model of car produced as a cost unit. If the business manufactures the chassis, body, engine, gearbox and the electrical system, these could also be treated as separate cost units.
- A carrier bag manufacturer has the same problems as a brick manufacturer: the costs identified with manufacturing one carrier bag are too small to be measured. Therefore, a suitable cost unit might be 1,000 bags of each type produced.
- Plumbers often work on a number of small jobs, which may vary from fitting a bathroom suite to replacing a tap washer. The plumber needs to know the cost of each job and so a suitable cost unit would be each job.
- In the case of a sports centre, managers need to know the separate cost of supplying badminton, squash, swimming, table tennis, etc. for a period of time. Therefore, a suitable cost unit would be each activity per hour.
- A hairdresser is likely to offer a number of standard services, such as cutting and styling, colouring, etc. Therefore, a suitable cost unit would be each standard service.
- A dating agency might use the cost of matching one couple.

> **Definition**
> A cost unit is a unit of production for which the management of an organization wishes to collect the costs incurred.
>
> Source: Law, 2010, p. 119

Figure 2.1 shows typical cost centres in a light bulb factory where costs are collected for a cost unit consisting of a batch of 12 light bulbs.

2.4 CLASSIFYING COSTS

Although it is useful to know the total expenditure for an accounting period, it is even more useful if the total is broken down into individual costs. This provides more detailed cost information for managers, who can use it for planning, controlling and decision making. Costs can be classified by:

- The *nature* of the cost, such as materials, rent and salaries.
- The *function* to which they relate, such as production costs, administrative expenses and distribution costs.
- Whether they are *product costs* which can be identified with the cost unit, or *period costs* which are deducted as expenses in the current period.
- Whether they are *direct costs*, which are costs that can be directly traced to a cost unit, or *indirect costs*, which cannot, although they may be traced directly to a cost centre.
- The *behaviour* of the cost and whether they are *variable costs*, which in total change in proportion with the level of production activity, or *fixed costs*, which are not changed by fluctuations in production levels.

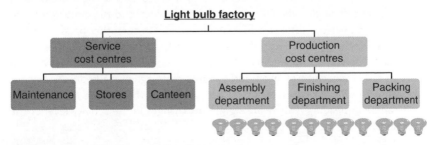

Figure 2.1 Typical cost centres in a factory

Direct costs are usually variable costs, and indirect costs are usually fixed costs. Examples of direct costs that are fixed costs are patents, licences and copyright relating to a particular product and some direct expenses such as the hire of a particular piece of equipment to produce a specific order.

Activity
Classify the following costs incurred in a manufacturing business into direct costs, indirect costs, variable costs and fixed costs:

Materials used in the product
Cost of renting the factory
Insurance of the factory
Depreciation
Maintenance of machinery
Canteen
Supervisors' salaries
Production workers' wages
Accountants' salaries

Materials can be traced to the product and therefore they can be classified as direct costs; so too are the production workers' wages, if they are paid according to the number of units produced. Rent, insurance, maintenance of machinery, canteen and the salaries cannot be identified with a particular product, but must be shared over a number of products. Therefore, these are classified as indirect costs. The same principles for classifying direct and indirect costs apply in the service sector.

You may have noticed that in the above example the direct costs are also variable costs, and the indirect costs are also fixed costs. The materials used in the product can be identified directly with the product, and the more items produced, the higher the total cost of materials used. On the other hand, rent and insurance for the period remain the same, regardless of the quantity of products produced. Therefore, these indirect costs are also classified as fixed costs. We will look at the importance of fixed and variable costs again in Chapter 6, but for the moment you need to remember that calculating the average total cost per unit can be misleading if there are significant changes in the activity level of the business.

Direct costs are classified into three categories as applicable:

- *Direct materials*, which are the cost of materials and components used to make the product.
- *Direct labour*, which are the costs of employing the workforce that converts the direct materials into the finished product.
- *Direct expenses*, which are not always incurred but include such costs as subcontract work or special tools and equipment bought for a particular order.

Once the individual direct costs have been calculated, they are aggregated to give what is known as the *prime cost*.

Definition
Direct costs are product costs that can be traced directly to a product or cost unit.

Source: Law, 2010, p. 145

The production overheads are the indirect production costs that cannot be traced to the cost unit. The production overheads are added to the direct costs to give the *production cost*. The non-production overheads are classified into three categories as applicable:

- *Administrative expenses*, which capture the cost of running the business.
- *Distribution costs*, which relate to the cost of promoting, selling and delivering the products and any after-sales services.
- *Research and development costs*, which capture expenditure on developing products and/or production processes.

These non-production overheads are added to the production overheads to arrive at the total cost.

Definition
Indirect costs are expenses that cannot be traced directly to a product or cost unit and are therefore overheads.

Source: Law, 2010, p. 230

Figure 2.2 summarises the typical classification of costs in the manufacturing industry.

Product direct costs (usually variable costs)	Indirect costs (usually fixed costs)
• Direct materials • Direct labour • Direct expenses	• Production overheads • Administrative expenses • Distribution costs • Research & development costs

Figure 2.2 Classifying direct and indirect costs

2.5   PREPARING A STATEMENT OF TOTAL COST

A *statement of total cost* can be prepared to show the total cost of a cost unit. It shows all the elements of cost and itemises the product direct costs plus a share of each of the indirect costs.

Activity

On 1 July, John Murphy started a business called Kingston Kitchens Ltd, which makes traditional country-style kitchen cabinets. At the end of the first week, the company had hand-crafted 10 cabinets and John had collected the following costs:

Direct materials	£440
Direct labour	£660
Production overheads	£200
Administrative expenses	£80
Distribution costs	£60

The company has no direct expenses or research and development costs. Using the following pro forma, calculate the total cost for the week.

Kingston Kitchens Ltd
Statement of total cost for w/e 7 July (10 units)

	£
Direct costs	
Direct materials	
Direct labour	——
Prime cost	
Production overheads	
Production cost	
Administrative expenses	
Distribution costs	
Total cost	═══

Your answer should look like this:

Kingston Kitchens Ltd
Statement of total cost for w/e 7 July (10 units)

	£
Direct costs	
Direct materials	440
Direct labour	660
Prime cost	1,100
Production overheads	200
Production cost	1,300
Administrative expenses	80
Distribution costs	60
Total cost	1,440

Activity
Now prepare a statement of total costs for 1 unit. As this is a very simple business, you can apportion the overheads by dividing them by the number of units produced.

Check your answer against the following solution.

Kingston Kitchens Ltd Statement of total cost (1 unit)	
	£
Direct costs	
Direct materials	44
Direct labour	66
Prime cost	110
Production overheads	20
Production cost	130
Administrative expenses	8
Distribution costs	6
Total cost	144

2.6   DETERMINING THE SELLING PRICE

Now John knows the total cost per week, he can ensure that the company has sufficient cash to support these costs. He also knows the cost per unit and this is very useful because the most important source of finance will be the revenue generated from selling the cabinets. The final step is to use the information from the statement of total cost per unit to determine the selling price of each cabinet.

> **Activity**
> Calculate the selling price if Kingston Kitchens Ltd wants to make a profit based on 40% of the production cost.

The total cost per unit is £144, to which you need to add the profit mark-up based on 40% of the production cost (£130 × 40% = £52) to arrive at a selling price of £196. In other words, if each cabinet is sold for £196, the total cost per unit of £144 will be covered and the company will make a profit of £52. The revised statement now looks like this:

Kingston Kitchens Ltd Statement of total cost (1 unit)	
	£
Direct costs	
Direct materials	44
Direct labour	66
Prime cost	110
Production overheads	20
Production cost	130
Administrative expenses	8
Distribution costs	6
Total cost	144
Profit (£130 × 40%)	52
Selling price	196

2.7 KEY POINTS

Cost accounting focuses on techniques for recording the cost of *cost units* and *cost centres*. A cost unit can be the final product, a sub-assembly or a batch of products. Production cost centres are those concerned with making a product, and service cost centres provide services to different parts of the business. Although it is useful to know the total expenditure for an accounting period, it is even more useful if it is broken down into individual costs and expenses. Classifying costs provides more detailed information for managers, who can use it for planning, controlling and decision making.

The statement of total cost we have examined in this chapter distinguishes between direct and indirect costs and is typically used in the manufacturing industry. The cost per unit is calculated by identifying the separate elements of direct cost and adding a share of the indirect costs. A profit mark-up can be added to establish the selling price per cost unit.

REVISION QUESTIONS

1. Explain the purpose of cost accounting and why it is important for managers to have cost information.
2. Describe the main classifications of cost.

3. Classify the following costs incurred in a manufacturing business into production costs, administrative expenses and distribution costs:

Factory rent
Insurance of office buildings
Electricity for powering machinery
Electricity for office lighting and heating
Tax and insurance of delivery vehicles
Depreciation of factory machinery
Depreciation of office equipment
Commission paid to sales team
Salaries paid to accounts office staff
Factory manager's salary
Delivery drivers' salaries
Factory security guards' salaries
Piecework wages paid to factory operatives
Salary paid to managing director's secretary
Salaries paid to factory canteen staff
Fees paid to advertising agency
Maintenance of machinery
Accounting software
Bonuses for factory staff
Training course for clerical staff

4. Portland Paving Ltd makes paving slabs sold to builders and garden centres. The business plans to produce 2,000 units over the next week and each unit requires the same amount of materials and takes the same time to produce. The expected costs for next week are as follows:

	£
Rent:	
Factory	1,000
Office	400
Lighting and heating:	
Factory	2,000
Office	800
Power	700

(Continued)

	£
Factory wages:	
Operators (piecework)	10,000
Maintenance staff (fixed)	1,500
Canteen staff (fixed)	2,500
Sand, cement and clay	6,000
Depreciation:	
Moulds	2,200
Factory fixtures and fittings	800
Office equipment	200
Office salaries	1,800
Sales team's salaries	2,200
Sales team's car expenses	1,600
Delivery expenses	500
Cement mixer repairs	900
Finishing paint	200
Delivery costs	800

Required
(a) Prepare a costing statement for Portland Paving Ltd that shows the elements of cost and calculates the total cost of producing 2,000 slabs.
(b) Interpret your statement by explaining the following terms:
   (i)   Direct costs
   (ii) Prime cost
   (iii) Production cost
   (iv) Indirect costs
   (v)   Total cost

5. Using the information for Portland Paving Ltd in Question 4, construct a statement that shows the elements of total cost for 1 unit. As this is a very simple business, you can apportion the overheads by dividing them by the number of units produced. In addition, calculate the selling price of 1 unit if the business requires a profit margin based on 50% of the production cost.

3
PRODUCT DIRECT COSTS

3.1 OBJECTIVES

Revenue expenditure can be classified as direct costs or indirect costs. This chapter focuses on direct costs, which are costs that can be traced directly to a product or cost unit. It examines two methods that are widely used to ascertain the cost of direct materials and value inventory. It also explains the main methods used to cost direct labour and direct expenses. After studying this chapter, you should be able to:

- Describe the main stages in controlling direct materials.
- Calculate the cost of direct materials using the first in, first out (FIFO) method.
- Calculate the cost of direct materials using the cost weighted average (CWA) method.
- Discuss the advantages and disadvantages of FIFO and CWA cost.
- Describe and apply the costing methods for direct labour and direct expenses.

3.2 MAIN STAGES IN MATERIAL CONTROL

In the previous chapter we looked at the various ways in which costs can be classified, and one way is to divide them into *direct costs* and *indirect costs*. *Direct costs* are costs that can be traced directly to a product or cost unit. They can be further classified into direct materials, direct labour and direct expenses.

In a manufacturing business, it is important that materials are available in the right place, at the right time and in the right quantities, and that all materials are properly accounted for. Therefore, a system of *material control* is essential to ensure that the production process is not delayed due to shortages of materials and the business does not tie up capital by storing higher levels of materials than necessary.

> **Definition**
> Materials are the production supplies of an organization that feature as revenue expenditure purchased from a third party ... Materials are not necessarily raw materials, but can include components and sub-assemblies used in the finished product.
>
> Source: Law, 2010, p. 278

The cost of materials purchased from a supplier is classified as revenue expenditure (costs that reduce profit and are written off as expenses in the accounting period). Materials can be divided into direct materials, which feature in the final product (such as wood and metal in furniture), and indirect materials, which are necessary to carry out production but do not feature in the final product (such as maintenance and cleaning materials). Initially, deliveries of materials are taken to the place where they will be stored (the stores) and records are kept of quantities received and prices paid. Depending on the size and conditions needed to hold the materials, the stores might be a small stockroom, a large warehouse or a secure yard from which the materials can be issued conveniently to production as required.

In a large business, the stores can carry many hundreds of different types of materials. Therefore the business requires an efficient and accurate system for recording and controlling the cost of materials. This can be either a manual or a computerised system. An effective system of material control ensures that:

- The correct materials are delivered.
- Materials are stored and issued only with proper authorisation.
- Production is charged with the cost of materials used.
- The inventory of materials in the stores is correctly valued.

Although material control systems can be designed to meet the needs of the business, a number of prime documents are used at each stage, as shown in Figure 3.1.

Many businesses have moved to just-in-time (JIT) manufacturing systems in which products are produced in time to meet demand, rather than producing products which are stored in case they are ordered. JIT systems greatly reduce or eliminate the need for large inventories of materials. Records of the quantity of goods in store should be maintained, and it is essential that a physical count is made because of the possibility of errors and theft. This is known as *stocktaking* and should be done at least annually. It requires a substantial amount of work and can be very disruptive. Some organisations use continuous stocktaking, where employees check a few items every day so that all inventories are checked at least once a year.

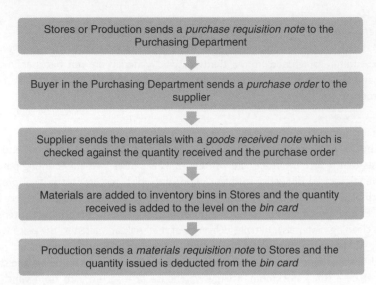

Figure 3.1 Main stages in material control

Copies of all prime documents are sent to the accountant so that they can be checked to ensure that materials have been properly ordered and received before the supplier's invoice is paid. The accountant also records the quantity and value of receipts and issues of materials, and the quantity and value of inventory. An *inventory account* is opened for each type of material and this is where the records are kept. These records provide the information needed to calculate the cost of materials used in each product or cost unit.

3.3   COSTING DIRECT MATERIALS

Direct materials are usually the main element of prime cost. The methods used for *costing direct materials* focus on the price at which materials are issued from stores to production. Calculating the cost of direct materials can be a problem. For example, it may not be possible to identify each issue of materials with the corresponding receipt into stores or it may be complicated by the fact that materials have been received on different dates and at a number of different purchase prices. Fluctuating prices may be due to a number of reasons, such as:

• A general rise in the price of goods or services due to inflation or a general lowering of prices due to deflation.

- Variations in exchange rates if materials are purchased overseas.
- Shortages in the supply of materials.
- Temporary discounts, such as special offers.

The method chosen for costing materials issued to production has implications for the cost of the product or cost unit and also for the value of inventory in the stores. Although some valuation methods might be satisfactory for management purposes, they are not all suitable for financial reporting purposes. Therefore, to avoid having to use one method for management accounting purposes and another for financial accounting purposes, most businesses choose a method that is suitable for both. There are four main methods:

- The *standard cost* method uses predetermined planned costs known as standard costs. The standard cost is derived from a standard quantity of materials allowed for the production of a specific cost unit at standard direct materials price. This method of standard costing is closely associated with a system of budgetary control (see Chapters 7 and 8).
- The *unit cost* method is the simplest method as far as actual costs are concerned, but it can only be used in a relatively small business where the cost of purchasing the specific direct materials used to produce the cost unit can be identified. This is the method we used in Chapter 2. However, as a business grows in terms of production volume and range of products, this is clearly no longer possible.
- The *first in, first out cost (FIFO cost)* is a method that uses the price of the earliest consignment of materials for all issues to production until the quantity received at that price has been issued, then the price of the next consignment.
- The *continuous weighted average cost (CWA cost)* is a method that uses the weighted average price of materials received which is recalculated every time a new consignment of that item is received. The weighted average price is calculated as:

$$\frac{\text{Total value of inventory}}{\text{Total quantity of inventory}}$$

Definitions

First in, first out cost (FIFO cost) is a method of valuing units of raw materials or finished goods issued from stock based on using the earliest unit value for pricing the issues until all [inventory] received at that price has been used up. The next latest price is then used for pricing the issues, and so on. Because the issues are based on a FIFO cost, the valuation of closing [inventory] is described as being on the same FIFO basis.

Source: Law, 2010, p. 192

> Continuous weighted average cost (CWA cost) is a method of valuing units of raw materials or finished goods issued from stock based on using the weighted-average price, which is recalculated every time a new consignment is received.
>
> Source: Collis, Holt and Hussey, 2012, p. 288

We will explain the FIFO and CWA cost methods by returning to the example of John Murphy's company, Kingston Kitchens Ltd.

Activity

You will remember from the previous chapter that Kingston Kitchens Ltd started making traditional country-style kitchen cabinets on 1 July. The goods received notes and the materials requisitions show the following receipts and issues of timber during the first three days. As you can see, John was able to negotiate a lower introductory price for the first delivery and then paid the regular price for the second delivery:

1 July	Received 50 units at £3.00 per unit
2 July	Received a further 50 units at £4.00 per unit
3 July	Issued 50 units to production

Complete the following record in the inventory account and calculate the cost of the 50 units issued to production on 3 July and 50 units remaining in inventory using the FIFO and CWA methods.

Timber inventory account

FIFO	Receipts			Issues			Inventory balance	
July	Quantity	Price	Value	Quantity	Price	Value	Quantity	Value
		£	£		£	£		£
1								
2								
3								
Total								

CWA	Receipts			Issues			Inventory balance	
July	Quantity	Price	Value	Quantity	Price	Value	Quantity	Value
		£	£		£	£		£
1								
2								
3								
Total								

Check your answer against the solution below.

Timber inventory account

FIFO	Receipts			Issues			Inventory balance	
July	Quantity	Price	Value	Quantity	Price	Value	Quantity	Value
		£	£		£	£		£
1	50	3.00	150.00				50	150.00
2	50	4.00	200.00				100	350.00
3				50	3.00	150.00	50	200.00
Total			350.00			150.00		

CWA	Receipts			Issues			Inventory balance	
July	Quantity	Price	Value	Quantity	Price	Value	Quantity	Value
		£	£		£	£		£
1	50	3.00	150.00				50	150.00
2	50	4.00	200.00				100	350.00
3				50	3.50	175.00	50	175.00
Total			350.00			175.00		

If you compare the results, you can see that the total cost of timber issued to production (and hence the cost of direct materials used in the product) and the value of the inventory remaining in stores vary according to the method used.

As the number of receipts and issues increased, John found it was more efficient to use a spreadsheet to record the movement of inventory and calculate the inventory balance. You may wish to do the same for the next activity.

Activity

John's usual supplier was unable to supply the timber that John wanted on 4 July and he decided to buy it at a higher price from another timber merchant. However, his regular supplier was able to meet his next order on 6 July. Using the following information, calculate the quantity and value of timber issued to production during the first week and the quantity and value of closing inventory at 7 July using the FIFO and CWA cost methods.

1 July	Received 50 units at £3.00 per unit
2 July	Received 50 units at £4.00 per unit
3 July	Issued 50 units to production
4 July	Received 10 units at £5.00 per unit
5 July	Issued 40 units to production
6 July	Received 40 units at £4.00 per unit
7 July	Issued 30 units to production

Check your answer against the following.

Timber inventory account

FIFO	Receipts			Issues			Inventory balance	
July	Quantity	Price	Value	Quantity	Price	Value	Quantity	Value
		£	£		£	£		£
1	50	3.00	150.00				50	150.00
2	50	4.00	200.00				100	350.00
3				50	3.00	150.00	50	200.00
4	10	5.00	50.00				60	250.00
5				40	4.00	160.00	20	90.00
6	40	4.00	160.00				60	250.00
7				10	4.00	40.00	50	210.00
7				10	5.00	50.00	40	160.00
7				10	4.00	40.00	30	120.00
Total			560.00			440.00		

CWA	Receipts			Issues			Inventory balance	
July	Quantity	Price	Value	Quantity	Price	Value	Quantity	Value
		£	£		£	£		£
1	50	3.00	150.00				50	150.00
2	50	4.00	200.00				100	350.00
3				50	3.50	175.00	50	175.00
4	10	5.00	50.00				60	225.00
5				40	3.75	150.00	20	75.00
6	40	4.00	160.00				60	235.00
7				30	3.92	117.50	30	117.50
Total			560.00			442.50		

The main thing to remember about using the CWA cost method is that you need to recalculate the average price at which inventory will be issued if a new consignment of that particular item has been received. This means calculating the new total value of inventory and dividing it by the new total quantity of inventory at that date. To find the cost of materials issued on 3 July you should have divided the inventory value of £350 by the quantity of inventory (100 units) to arrive at £3.50 per unit. Another consignment of timber is received on 4 July, so the cost of materials issued on 5 July is the new inventory value of £225 divided by the new quantity of inventory (60 units), which is £3.75 per unit. Since further timber is received on 6 July, you need to divide the new inventory value of £235 by the new quantity of inventory (60 units), which is £3.92 per unit (rounded to the nearest 1p). This is the new weighted average price used for the materials issued on 7 July.

In the previous chapter we looked at the total costs for Kingston Kitchens Ltd for the week ending 7 July in order to explain the different elements of total cost. In the above activity we have focused on how the cost of direct materials is calculated. You can see from the total cost statement below that John Murphy used a figure of £440 as the cost of the direct materials issued to production during the week ending 7 July.

Kingston Kitchens Ltd
Total cost w/e 7 July (10 cabinets)

	£
Direct costs	
Direct materials	440
Direct labour	660
Prime cost	1,100
Production overheads	200
Production cost	1,300
Indirect costs	
Administrative expenses	80
Distribution costs	60
Total cost	1,440

If you look at the same figure in the two sets of inventory accounts you have prepared for this activity, you will see that John must have been using the FIFO method, because the CWA method results in a higher figure of £442.50. Both figures are correct and this is another example of why managers need to have some understanding of the techniques used by accountants in order to make informed decisions.

3.4   ADVANTAGES AND DISADVANTAGES OF FIFO AND CWA

There are a number of advantages and disadvantages to the FIFO and CWA cost methods. Since the cost information provided is likely to be used for financial reporting purposes, it is important that the business chooses the most appropriate method and uses it consistently in order to aid comparability.

> **Activity**
> Compare the FIFO and CWA cost methods by drawing up lists of the advantages and disadvantages of each.

You may have thought of some of the following pros and cons of the two methods.

Advantages of FIFO cost

- It is acceptable to financial accountants in the UK and also to HM Revenue and Customs. This means that in addition to being used for management accounting purposes, it can be used for financial reporting and computing profits for taxation purposes.
- It is a logical choice if it coincides with the order in which inventory is physically issued to production. For example, if the inventory consists of perishable materials or materials that have a finite life for some other reason, it makes sense to issue those that have been stored the longest first. This avoids the possibility of deterioration, obsolescence and waste.
- It charges the cost of direct materials against profits in the same order as costs are incurred.
- The value of inventory at end of period is close to current prices.
- When prices are rising, the cost of materials issued is lower and the value of closing inventory is higher under FIFO than under the CWA, so FIFO cost maximises gross profit in the statement of comprehensive income.

Disadvantages of FIFO cost

- It is complex and an arithmetical burden, even when a spreadsheet is used.
- The cost of direct materials issued to production is based on historical prices.

Advantages of CWA cost

- It is acceptable to financial accountants in the UK and also to HM Revenue and Customs. This means that in addition to being used for management accounting purposes, it can be used for financial reporting and for computing profits for taxation purposes.
- It is a logical choice if it coincides with the way in which inventory is physically issued to production. For example, if inventory consists of volume and liquid materials (for example, building materials or chemicals), an averaging method makes sense as it may not be possible to differentiate between old and new inventory held in bulk storage containers.
- It takes account of quantities purchased and changing prices.
- It takes account of prices relating to previous periods.
- It can be relatively simple to calculate by entering the quantity and pricing information from the goods received notes and purchase orders (or stores requisitions) into a spreadsheet or specialist software package.

• It smoothes out the impact of price changes in the statement of comprehensive income.

Disadvantages of CWA cost

• Prices of materials issued to production must be recalculated every time a new consignment is received.
• Prices of materials issued may not match any of the prices actually paid.
• Value of closing inventory lags behind current prices if prices are rising.

3.5   COSTING DIRECT LABOUR

Direct labour is the second element of prime cost and relates to expenditure on wages paid to the workforce which can be traced directly to the products or cost unit. The methods for *costing direct labour* are closely related to the type of pay scheme. These are:

• *Piecework schemes*, which are used when workers are paid an agreed amount for each unit produced or piecework time is paid for each unit produced.
• *Time-based schemes*, which are used when workers are paid a basic rate per time period.
• *Incentive schemes*, which are used when a time allowance is given for each job and a bonus is paid for any time saved.

In piecework schemes wages can be calculated using the following formula:

$$\text{Units produced} \times \text{Rate of pay per cost unit}$$

For example, if an employee is paid £1.50 per cost unit and produces 240 units in a week, his or her weekly pay will be £360. This method works only where all units are identical. If the employee produces a number of different units a conversion factor must be applied. As a piecework system is based on time spent on production, a standard time allowance is given for each unit to arrive at a total of piecework hours. Perhaps the same employee is allowed 15 minutes to produce 1 unit of product A (a simple electronic circuit board) and 30 minutes to produce 1 unit of product B (a more complex electronic circuit board). If the employee produces 40 units of product A and 60 units of product B and is paid £10 per hour, his or her pay can be calculated as follows:

Product	Number of units	Time allowance per unit	Total hours
A	40	0.25 hours	10
B	60	0.50 hours	30
			40
		Pay (£10 × 40)	£400

Calculating pay for time-based schemes is straightforward. A system is required to ensure that the employee is properly appointed and, if necessary, a procedure is in place to record the employee's attendance at the workplace. In many jobs it is assumed that the employee is present unless absence is specifically reported. The records from the clock cards and/or time sheets are then used as the basis for calculating pay.

Incentive schemes are usually introduced where workers are paid under a time-based scheme. There are various types of scheme in operation, but most are based on setting a target for output and actual performance is compared with the target. If actual performance exceeds the target, employees receive a payment for their efficiency. This payment is a proportion of the savings made by the business because of the increased efficiency and therefore the labour cost per unit should be lower. It is important to remember that a performance-based scheme cannot be used if the output cannot be measured reliably. It would also be preferable to adopt a time-based method of remuneration where the quality of output is important, even though output might be easy to measure. This would avoid the danger of quality deteriorating as workers strive to achieve higher levels of output that bring them increased monetary rewards.

Activity

John Murphy employs Chris, Mike and Adam in the workshop of Kingston Kitchens Ltd. As Chris and Mike are apprentices, they are paid £10 per hour, but Adam has qualifications and experience and is paid £20 per hour. Their time sheets for the week ending 7 July show that Chris spent 25 hours, Mike spent 15 hours and Adam spent 10 hours on the kitchen cabinets made that week. John's accountant, who manages the payroll, estimates that the additional employer's costs incurred for pension contributions, holiday pay, etc. amount to 10% of the wages paid. Use this information to calculate the direct labour cost for the 10 cabinets produced.

Check your answer against the following workings.

	Hours	Rate per hour	Total
		£	£
Chris	25	10.00	250
Mike	15	10.00	150
Adam	10	20.00	200
			600
Employer's costs (£600 × 10%)			60
Total direct labour costs			660

If you look at the total cost statement for Kingston Kitchens Ltd reproduced below, the direct labour costs are the most significant element of the direct costs for this business. Therefore, they are a key element of the prime costs for the week. One way in which John Murphy controls the direct labour costs in his business is by ensuring that employees complete their time sheets accurately and differentiate between time spent on making the cabinets and time spent on general tasks, such as clearing up and maintenance. Indeed, both Chris and Adam spend part of the day on general tasks and Adam spends time supervising the apprentices and helping John with production planning. Since this time cannot be identified directly with the products, the wages bill for this part of their jobs is included with the production overheads in the costing statement.

Kingston Kitchens Ltd Total cost w/e 7 July (10 cabinets)	
	£
Direct costs	
Direct materials	440
Direct labour	660
Prime cost	1,100
Production overheads	200
Production cost	1,300
Administrative expenses	80
Distribution costs	60
Total cost	1,440

You should not be misled into thinking that methods for costing direct labour are used only in manufacturing businesses. For example, professional firms of solicitors and accountants usually complete time sheets so that each client can be billed for the services they receive. In all organisations it is necessary to have a system to ensure that employees are properly remunerated for their contribution. In many service organisations, some form of bonus or profit-sharing scheme is likely to exist and this requires more detailed information to be kept.

3.6   COSTING DIRECT EXPENSES

Apart from direct materials and direct labour, a business may have some *direct expenses*. Examples of direct expenses include subcontract work or hiring special equipment for a particular job. For example, John Murphy might decide to continue making standard kitchen cabinets, but also offer them with a paint finish as chosen by the customer. He may decide to subcontract the painting to an expert. The cost of this extra work is not a direct material, as the paint is not purchased or owned by Kingston Kitchens Ltd; nor is it direct labour, as the painter is not on the payroll. Nevertheless, the cost can be traced directly to a product. Therefore it is classified as a direct expense.

The main method for *costing direct expenses* to a product or cost unit is based on the amount shown in the relevant invoice. If it is not possible to trace the expense to a particular cost unit, the amount is simply added to the production overheads.

3.7   KEY POINTS

A system of material control is needed to ensure that the correct materials are delivered, and that they are stored and issued only when authorised, the cost of materials used is charged to production, and inventory is valued correctly. The main methods used for costing direct materials relate to the prices used for issuing materials to production. FIFO cost uses the price of the oldest consignment for issues until quantities at that price are exhausted, then the next price. CWA cost uses the weighted average price, which is recalculated every time a consignment is received. These two methods are both acceptable for financial reporting purposes in the UK.

The methods used for costing direct labour are linked to the method of remuneration. If the amount can be traced to a particular cost unit, the costing method for direct expenses is based on the amount shown in the invoice.

REVISION QUESTIONS

1. Describe the main stages in controlling direct materials.
2. Compare and contrast the advantages and disadvantages of the FIFO and CWA cost methods.
3. Monica's wages are based on piecework and she is paid £10 per piecework hour. Calculate her pay for a 36-hour week in which she produces the following units:

Product	Number of units	Time allowance per unit
A	12	0.8 hours
B	30	0.6 hours
C	24	0.5 hours

4. Butler Ltd makes stylish, stainless steel cutlery. On 1 December the inventory records show 500 kg of metal alloy, which is valued at £2.00 per kg. The goods received notes and materials requisitions show the following receipts and issues during the month:

2 December	Issued 450 kg to production
7 December	Received 550 kg at £2.10 per kg
8 December	Issued 500 kg to production
14 December	Received 600 kg at £2.20 per kg
15 December	Issued 600 kg to production
30 December	Received 500 kg at £2.30 per kg
31 December	Issued 100 kg to production

Required

(a) Prepare the metal alloy inventory account for December using:

   (i) FIFO cost
   (ii) CWA cost

   Interpret each inventory account by indicating the cost of metal alloy issued to production during December and the quantity and value of closing inventory at 31 December.

(b) Discuss the advantages and disadvantages of the two methods and conclude by recommending which method Butler Ltd should adopt, giving at least five reasons.

5. The records for September show the movement of inventory for tomatoes, the main ingredient used in the pasta sauces made by Sergio's Sauces Ltd.

| September | Receipts | | Issues |
	Quantity (tonnes)	Price per tonne £	Quantity (tonnes)
1	1,000	5.00	
2	1,000	5.50	
3			750
14			750
15	1,000	6.00	
16			750
29	1,000	6.50	
30			750

Required

(a) Prepare the tomato inventory account for September using:

   (i)   FIFO cost
   (ii) CWA cost

   Interpret each inventory account by indicating the cost of tomatoes used in the product during September and the inventory balance in terms of quantity and value at 30 September.

(b) Identify which of the two costing methods would give the higher gross profit for the month, explaining your reasons.

4

ABSORPTION COSTING

4.1 OBJECTIVES

Revenue expenditure can be classified as direct costs or indirect costs. This chapter focuses on absorption costing, which is the traditional method used to charge indirect costs to the cost unit and calculate the total cost per unit. After studying this chapter, you should be able to:

- Describe the main purposes of absorption costing.
- Explain the main stages in absorption costing.
- Construct a production overhead analysis.
- Calculate the total cost of a cost unit using absorption costing.
- Discuss the problems of under-absorption and over-absorption.

4.2 MAIN STAGES IN ABSORPTION COSTING

In the previous chapter we looked at the various ways in which costs can be classified and one way is to divide them into *direct costs* and *indirect costs*. *Indirect costs* are the *overheads* of the business that cannot be traced directly to a product or cost unit. They can be further classified into production overheads, administrative overheads, distribution overheads, and research and development overheads. In many businesses these costs are very high and *absorption costing* is the traditional method used to charge them to the product and calculate the total cost for each cost unit.

> **Definitions**
>
> Absorption costing is the cost accounting system in which the overheads of an organization are charged to the production by means of the process of absorption. Costs are first allocated or apportioned to the cost centres, where they are absorbed into the cost unit using absorption rates.
>
> An overhead absorption rate (OAR) is the rate or rates calculated in an absorption costing system in advance of an accounting period for the purpose of charging the overheads to the production of that period.
>
> Source: Law, 2010, p. 2

The total of the product direct costs is the *prime cost* and the addition of the production overheads (the indirect costs of production) gives the *production cost*. While the production cost of the cost unit is needed primarily for planning and controlling the production costs and for valuing inventory, the total cost is needed to determine the selling price. The following activity examines this in more detail.

> **Activity**
>
> John Murphy's company, Kingston Kitchens Ltd, is thriving. During the first year, the workshop made 1,000 kitchen cabinets with the same design and specification. Production overheads for the year were £20,000; direct materials for each cabinet were £50 and direct labour costs for each cabinet were £80. What is the production cost of 1 cabinet?

You should have had no problem in deciding that the total direct costs are £130 (direct materials £50 + direct labour £80). However, the total cost must include a fair share of the production overheads, but what is a fair share? As the business is making only one product and they are all the same, a fair method would be to divide the production overheads by the total number of units produced:

$$\frac{£20,000}{1,000} = £20$$

The following costing statement shows these calculations.

Kingston Kitchens Ltd Production cost (1 cabinet)	
	£
Direct costs	
Direct materials	50
Direct labour	80
Prime cost	130
Production overheads	20
Production cost	150

As a business grows, it is likely to become more complex, and the owner(s) may decide to organise it into functional departments. In a manufacturing business, some will be production departments and others will be service departments, such as maintenance, storage or canteen facilities, administration, sales, procurement, distribution, etc. A larger business is likely to have a range of products, with each cost unit spending a different amount of time in the production department and making different demands on resources. Absorption costing seeks to provide answers to two practical problems:

• How to share the total overheads of the business over the various production cost centres.
• How to share the overheads for a particular production cost centre over the various products passing through it.

> **Activity**
> Was the method used by Kingston Kitchens Ltd in the previous activity a solution to the first or the second of these problems?

It was a solution to the second problem because we were looking at a small organisation with only one production department or workshop. By dividing the total overheads by the number of kitchen cabinets produced, we shared the production overheads over the products passing through the production department. Usually we have to solve the first problem before we can tackle the second.

The main stages in absorption costing are shown in Figure 4.1.

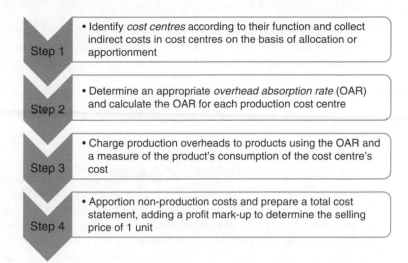

Step 1
• Identify *cost centres* according to their function and collect indirect costs in cost centres on the basis of allocation or apportionment

Step 2
• Determine an appropriate *overhead absorption rate* (OAR) and calculate the OAR for each production cost centre

Step 3
• Charge production overheads to products using the OAR and a measure of the product's consumption of the cost centre's cost

Step 4
• Apportion non-production costs and prepare a total cost statement, adding a profit mark-up to determine the selling price of 1 unit

Figure 4.1 Main stages in absorption costing

4.3 ALLOCATING AND APPORTIONING PRODUCTION OVERHEADS

In Chapter 2, we explained that one way in which costs can be classified is by *nature*. When indirect costs are classified by nature, they fall into two main groups. If the overheads can be wholly identified with one particular cost centre, the accountant can use a process called *cost allocation*. If the overheads cannot be identified with a single cost centre, the accountant needs to find a way of sharing them over all the cost centres benefiting from them. This process is known as *cost apportionment*. For example, factory rent might be apportioned over the production cost centres on the basis of the proportion of space each department occupies in the factory.

A *production overhead analysis* is prepared which lists the total overheads classified by nature and shows how they are apportioned across the production cost centres. The following activity illustrates this process.

Activity
Denim Blue Ltd makes jeans. It has two cost centres: the cutting department where the denim is cut out by machine, and the stitching department where the jeans are sewn and finished. Some of the production overheads have been

(Continued)

allocated to the two cost centres from information available within the business, but the remainder must be apportioned in some way. The following information should help you decide a fair way of sharing them between the two departments.

	Total	Cutting department	Stitching department
Production area	400 sq metres	250 sq metres	150 sq metres
Number of employees	20	5	15
Value of machinery	£120,000	£100,000	£20,0000
Value of inventory	£120,000	£40,000	£80,0000

First, you need to decide the basis on which to apportion the production overheads, and then calculate the portion that will be borne by each cost centre. The indirect materials and indirect labour used in production have already been allocated and entered on the pro forma below. The rent has also been apportioned to show you the method. Rent is best apportioned on the basis of the area occupied. The total area is 250 + 150 = 400 sq metres and the rent is £12,000. Therefore, the rent can be apportioned as follows:

$$\text{Cutting department: } \frac{250}{400} \text{ sq metres} \times £12,000 = £7,500$$

$$\text{Stitching department: } \frac{150}{400} \text{ sq metres} \times £12,000 = £4,500$$

Denim Blue Ltd Production overhead analysis				
Overhead	Total	Basis of apportionment	Cutting department	Stitching department
	£		£	£
Indirect materials	40,000	Allocated	17,500	22,500
Indirect labour	17,100	Allocated	4,200	12,900
Rent and rates	12,000	Area	7,500	4,500
Lighting and heating	4,000			

Depreciation on machinery	9,000		
Supervisors' salaries	22,000		
Insurance	900		
Total	105,000		

After deciding on a fair way of apportioning the production overheads, the calculations are not difficult. Check your completed analysis against the following solution.

		Denim Blue Ltd Production overhead analysis		
Overhead	Total	Basis of apportionment	Cutting department	Stitching department
	£		£	£
Indirect materials	40,000	Allocated	17,500	22,500
Indirect labour	17,100	Allocated	4,200	12,900
Rent and rates	12,000	Area	7,500	4,500
Lighting and heating	4,000	Area	2,500	1,500
Depreciation on machinery	9,000	Value of machinery	7,500	1,500
Supervisors' salaries	22,000	No. of employees	5,500	16,500
Insurance	900	Value of inventory	300	600
Total	105,000		45,000	60,000

Your answer will differ from the above if you decided to use different bases of apportionment, so we will look at the reasons for the choices we made. Both rent and lighting and heating would seem to be best shared on the basis of the area occupied by each cost centre. Depreciation is clearly related to the value of the machinery used in each cost centre. Deciding on the best way to apportion the supervisors' salaries is more difficult. In the absence of any other information, we have assumed that their salaries are related to the number of employees under their supervision. You might argue that they could be related to floor space and in some circumstances you would be right. Finally, the insurance of inventory is based on its value and therefore has been allocated accordingly.

Production overhead	Basis of apportionment
Rent and rates	Area or volume
Lighting and heating	Area or volume
Insurance of buildings	Area
Insurance of inventory	Value of inventory
Insurance of machinery	Value of machinery
Depreciation on machinery	Value of machinery
Power for machinery	Machine hours, horsepower or horsepower per hour
Supervisors' salaries	Number of employees
Canteen	Number of employees

Table 4.1 Main bases for apportioning production overheads

Finding a fair way to apportion overheads is a major problem in many organisations and it is important to remember that the methods of apportionment are arbitrary. Nevertheless, the method chosen should be reasonable. The costs should be relatively easy to obtain from the records of the business and relate to the manner in which they are incurred by the cost centre benefiting from their use. Finally, they should reflect the use by the cost centre of the resources represented by the overhead. Later in this chapter we will be looking at the problem of service cost centres, but at this stage we will concentrate on how to allocate or apportion production overheads to our two production departments. Table 4.1 shows some commonly used bases of apportionment.

4.4　CALCULATING THE PRODUCTION OVERHEAD ABSORPTION RATE

Returning to our example of Denim Blue Ltd, we now know that the total production overheads are £45,000 for the cutting department and £60,000 for the finishing department. Next we must decide on an appropriate *overhead absorption rate (OAR)* which we will use to share the production overheads between all the jeans passing through the two production cost centres. The choice of absorption rate depends on the basis of apportionment and the resources used. We will examine the following:

- The cost unit overhead absorption rate.
- The direct labour hour overhead absorption rate.
- The machine hour overhead absorption rate.

The *cost unit overhead absorption rate* is the simplest method and involves dividing the production overheads for each production cost centre by the number of cost units passing through them. We applied this in the Kingston Kitchens Ltd example. In a more complex business there may be more than one production cost centre and a different overhead absorption rate will be needed for each. For example, Denim Blue Ltd makes two styles of jeans: classic jeans and designer jeans. In one year, 4,000 classic jeans are made and 1,000 designer jeans, making a total of 5,000 cost units. Using the cost unit overhead absorption rate, we will now calculate the amount of the overheads that will be borne by each pair of jeans. This requires some care, as we need to remember that each pair of jeans must pass through the cutting department and the stitching department. Therefore, a separate overhead absorption rate per pair of jeans must be calculated for each cost centre and then aggregated.

	Cutting department	Stitching department
Cost unit overhead absorption rate:		
$\dfrac{\text{Cost centre overheads}}{\text{Total cost units}}$	$\dfrac{£45,000}{5,000} = £9.00$	$\dfrac{£60,000}{5,000} = £12.00$

The absorption rate will be £21.00 (£9.00 + £12.00). This means that every pair of jeans will absorb £21.00 of the production overheads incurred in running these two production cost centres.

However, it would be unfair to charge the same overhead to the different styles of jeans, since the more expensive designer jeans use more of the resources. It would be fairer if the product that uses more of the resources bears more of the overhead. The company could use an overhead absorption rate based on the time an employee spends working on the product (the direct labour hour rate) or on how long the product is on a machine (the machine hour rate).

Activity

Calculate the hourly overhead absorption rate for each production department of Denim Blue Ltd. You can choose to base the rate on direct labour hours or on machine hours. The following table gives details of the direct labour hours and machine hours required in each department to make 5,000 pairs of jeans.

	Cutting department	Stitching department
Direct labour hours	10,000	30,000
Machine hours	40,000	5,000

To calculate the direct labour hour overhead absorption rate for each cost centre, you need to divide the overhead by the total direct labour hours and add them together. If you decided to calculate the machine hours overhead absorption rate, for each cost centre, you should have divided the overhead by the total number of machine hours and added them together. Check your answer against the following workings.

	Cutting department	Stitching department
Direct labour hour overhead absorption rate:		
$\dfrac{\text{Cost centre overheads}}{\text{Total direct labour hours}}$	$\dfrac{£45,000}{10,000} = £4.50$	$\dfrac{£60,000}{30,000} = £2.00$
Machine hour overhead absorption rate:		
$\dfrac{\text{Cost centre overheads}}{\text{Total machine hours}}$	$\dfrac{£45,000}{40,000} = £1.13$	$\dfrac{£60,000}{5,000} = £12.00$

Other types of overhead absorption rate are often based on a percentage, but we will concentrate on the three methods we have illustrated as they are widely used and illustrate the main principles. The following table summarises the information we have so far.

	Cutting department	Stitching department
Total overheads	£45,000	£60,000
Number of cost units	5,000	5,000
Direct labour hours	10,000	30,000
Machine hours	40,000	5,000
Cost unit overhead absorption rate	£9.00	£12.00
Direct labour hour overhead absorption rate	£4.50	£2.00
Machine hour overhead absorption rate	£1.13	£12.00

Although we have calculated three different types of overhead rate for Denim Blue Ltd, only one rate will be used in each department. You can see that, since each one produces a different absorption rate, it is important that the management accountant uses the fairest rate for each cost centre, bearing in mind that the same rate need not be used in both departments. We have already pointed out that it would be unfair to use the cost unit absorption rate because the two types of jeans use unequal amounts of resources. With the other two rates, we need to consider the main sources of expenditure in each department by examining the overhead costs. In the cutting department, you can see that the overheads have been incurred mainly in terms of machine hours. Therefore this is the most appropriate basis for calculating the overhead absorption rate for that cost centre. However, in the finishing department, the work is mainly manual; therefore, the direct labour hour rate is the most appropriate overhead absorption rate to use for this cost centre.

We now have the information needed to allocate and absorb the production overheads into the cost unit, but we must not forget to charge for the direct materials and direct labour used in making the jeans. The following information is available:

	Classic jeans	Designer jeans
Direct materials	£50	£80
Direct labour	£20	£40
Cutting department machine hours	7	12
Stitching department direct labour hours	5	10

We can now calculate the production cost incurred in making each type of jeans.

Production cost per unit		
	Classic jeans	Designer jeans
	£	£
Direct costs		
Direct materials	50.00	80.00
Direct labour	20.00	40.00
Prime cost	70.00	120.00
Production overheads		
Cutting department (hours x £1.13 per machine hour)	7.91	13.56
Stitching department (hours x £2.00 per direct labour hour)	10.00	20.00
	17.91	33.56
Production cost	87.91	153.56

You may think that calculating a different overhead absorption rate for each production department is a very complex activity and it would be far simpler to calculate a factory-wide absorption rate. For example, if a factory had total overheads of £1m and there were 250,000 direct labour hours worked during the period, the overhead absorption rate would be £4.00 per labour hour in all departments. However, such a method is likely to generate incorrect data, except in a very simple production system. If there are a number of departments, and products spend unequal amounts of time in each department, separate departmental overhead absorption rates must be calculated. If this is not done, some products will receive a higher overhead charge than they should fairly bear and others a lower charge. This will make it difficult for management to control costs and make decisions on pricing and alternative production systems.

4.5   APPORTIONING SERVICE COST CENTRE OVERHEADS

In addition to production cost centres, most businesses also have cost centres that provide services to other cost centres. Examples of *service cost centres* include departments associated with the production areas, such as maintenance, stores and canteen, and others which are not, such as administration and distribution. The first stage is to calculate the total production cost as before and then apportion the service cost centres associated with production on a fair basis. We cannot illustrate this with Denim Blue Ltd because the company does not have any service cost centres. Therefore, we will return to the example of Kingston Kitchens Ltd.

Activity

Kingston Kitchens Ltd has expanded and now makes kitchen cabinets of different sizes. Instead of a single production department, John has found it more efficient to divide the work into separate stages and there are now three departments, each of which is a separate cost centre. The following information is available.

	Joinery department	Finishing department	Maintenance department
Area	200 sq metres	200 sq metres	100 sq metres
Number of employees	12	16	4
Value of machinery	£250,000	£100,000	£50,000

The maintenance department provides services to the two production departments. Complete the production overhead analysis below by showing the basis of apportionment and the overhead to be borne by each cost centre. The allocated overheads have been entered for you. Once you have calculated the subtotal for the three cost centres, you must apportion the costs of the service cost centre (the maintenance department) over the two production departments on an appropriate basis.

Kingston Kitchens Ltd
Production overhead analysis

Overhead	Total	Basis of apportionment	Joinery department	Finishing department	Maintenance department
	£		£	£	£
Indirect materials	10,000	Allocated	6,000	3,000	1,000
Indirect labour	31,500	Allocated	4,000	8,000	19,500
Rent and rates	20,000				
Electricity	5,000				
Depreciation on machinery	40,000				
Supervisors' salaries	36,000				
	142,500		____	____	____
Apportioned service costs	–				
Total	142,500		____	____	____

Your completed production overhead analysis should look like this:

Kingston Kitchens Ltd
Production overhead analysis

Overhead	Total	Basis of apportionment	Joinery department	Finishing department	Maintenance department
	£		£	£	£
Indirect materials	10,000	Allocated	6,000	3,000	1,000
Indirect labour	31,500	Allocated	4,000	8,000	19,500
Rent and rates	20,000	Area	8,000	8,000	4,000

(Continued)

Electricity	5,000	Area	2,000	2,000	1,000
Depreciation on machinery	40,000	Value of machinery	25,000	10,000	5,000
Supervisors' salaries	36,000	No. of employees	13,500	18,000	4,500
	142,500		58,500	49,000	35,000
Apportioned service costs	–	Value of machinery	25,000	10,000	(35,000)
Total	142,500		83,500	59,000	–

The indirect costs of £35,000 represent the cost of running the maintenance department. These costs have been apportioned to the two production departments on the basis of the value of the machinery in each. (The value of the machinery in the maintenance department itself is ignored.) The total cost of machinery in the production departments is £250,000 + £100,000 = £350,000. Therefore, the maintenance department overheads can be apportioned as follows:

$$\text{Joinery department:} \quad \frac{£250,000}{£350,000} \times £35,000 = £25,000$$

$$\text{Finishing department:} \quad \frac{£100,000}{£350,000} \times £35,000 = £10,000$$

Continuing this example, the overhead absorption rate in the joinery department is based on 10,000 machine hours and in the finishing department on 30,000 direct labour hours. We can now calculate the two overhead absorption rates in the joinery and finishing departments. This is done by dividing the total cost centre overhead for the period by the number of units of the basis of absorption; in this case, the machine hours in the joinery department and the direct labour hours in the finishing department:

$$\text{Joinery department:} \quad \frac{£83,500}{10,000} = £8.35 \text{ per machine hour}$$

$$\text{Finishing department:} \quad \frac{£59,000}{30,000} = £1.97 \text{ per direct labour hour}$$

Suppose a customer places an order for a kitchen cabinet for which the direct costs are direct materials £80.00 and direct labour £50.00. It is estimated that the cabinet will require 8 machine hours in the joinery department and 10 labour hours in the finishing department. The total production cost is calculated as follows.

Kingston Kitchens Ltd Production cost (1 cabinet)	
	£
Direct costs	
Direct materials	80.00
Direct labour	50.00
Prime cost	130.00
Production overheads	
Joinery department (8 hours x £8.35)	66.80
Finishing department (10 hours x £1.97)	19.70
	86.50
Production cost	216.50

In order to find out the total cost per unit, we need to add a proportion of the non-production overheads. In this example, these consist of the administrative overheads and distribution overheads. The data for the period is as follows.

	£		£
Direct costs	87,500	Administrative overheads	18,250
Production overheads	142,500	Distribution overheads	27,750
Total production cost	230,000	Total non-production overheads	46,000

A simple method for apportioning non-production overheads to a cost unit is to add a percentage representing the proportion of non-production costs to production costs. This is an arbitrary measure as there is no theoretical justification for a relationship between these two costs. The formula is:

$$\frac{\text{Non-production overheads}}{\text{Production cost}} \times 100$$

Substituting the figures in the formula:

$$\frac{£46,000}{£230,000} \times 100 = 20\% \text{ of the production cost } (£216.50 \times 20\%) = £43.30$$

Now we have all the figures we need to calculate the total cost of the cabinet. This is primarily of use to management for determining the selling price, since inventory valuation and controlling production costs do not require the inclusion of the non-production costs.

Production cost (1 cabinet)	
	£
Direct costs	
Direct materials	80.00
Direct labour	50.00
Prime cost	130.00
Production overheads	
Joinery department (8 hours × £8.35)	66.80
Finishing department (10 hours × £1.97)	19.70
Production cost	216.50
Non-production overheads (Production cost × 20%)	43.30
Total cost	259.80

4.6   UNDER–ABSORPTION AND OVER–ABSORPTION

There are no rules and regulations governing management accounting because the information is intended for internal users. One advantage of this is that information about costs can be produced for future accounting periods. In absorption costing the cost information is based on budgeted (predetermined) costs. The actual costs are not used because the collection, analysis and absorption of overheads to cost units takes a considerable time and the actual figures are not available until the end of the accounting period (typically a week, a month or a quarter of a year).

The budgeted costs will take account of a number of factors. For example, the planned level of activity will need to be decided, the number of machine hours and labour hours must be estimated and forecasts made of the likely overhead costs. This allows a *predetermined overhead absorption rate* to be calculated at the beginning of the accounting period, which is then applied throughout that period.

> **Activity**
> What problems do you think might arise from using a predetermined overhead rate instead of an actual rate?

You may have thought of the following problems:

- The actual overhead may differ from the budgeted overhead.
- The actual absorption rate may differ from the budgeted absorption rate.
- A combination of these factors.

Such problems can have serious consequences. If a business has been invoicing customers on the basis of a budgeted overhead rate that is wrong, it could have a significant impact on profit. When the budgeted overheads are higher than the actual overheads for the period, the variance is known as *over-absorption* because too much overhead has been charged. When the budgeted overheads are lower than the actual overheads, the variance is known as *under-absorption* because too little overhead has been charged. The amount under-absorbed represents the non-recovery of some of the overhead and reduces profit for the period.

4.7   KEY POINTS

Absorption costing is the traditional cost accounting system in which each cost unit is charged with a fair share of the indirect costs or overheads. A production overhead analysis shows the allocation or apportionment of the indirect costs to the cost centres on a fair basis. Total indirect costs from any service cost centres are allocated or apportioned to the production cost centres. The resulting indirect costs from each production cost centre are absorbed into the cost unit using a suitable overhead absorption rate. In a simple business with only one product, the rate can be based on the number of cost units passing through the production cost centre. In a more complex business, it is usually based on time, such as direct labour hours or machine hours.

Absorption costing provides the data needed to prepare a total costing statement for each cost unit that shows the different elements of direct and indirect cost. The selling price is calculated by adding a profit element. If the budgeted overheads are higher than the actual overheads for the period, the variance is known as over-absorption. Conversely, if the budgeted overheads are lower than the actual overheads, the variance is known as under-absorption. The amount under-absorbed represents the non-recovery of some of the overhead and reduces profit for the period.

REVISION QUESTIONS

1. Describe the main stages for calculating the total cost per unit under an absorption costing system.
2. Explain what it means to allocate, apportion and absorb indirect costs.
3. Discuss the advantages and disadvantages of using an absorption costing system for calculating the total cost of a product.
4. Jeremy Fernando is the owner of Fernando Garden Furniture Ltd, a company that makes Sri Lankan teak garden furniture. The following table shows the budgeted monthly production overheads.

Production overheads	
	£
Indirect materials	24,500
Indirect labour	54,500
Rent and rates	26,000
Lighting and heating	4,000
Depreciation on machinery	36,000
Supervisors' salaries	42,000

The company has two production cost centres and one service cost centre, details of which are shown opposite.

	Machine department	Assembly department	Maintenance department
Allocation of indirect materials	12,000	10,000	2,500
Allocation of indirect labour costs	14,000	18,000	22,500
Area (sq metres)	500	400	100
Value of machinery (£)	300,000	100,000	50,000
Number of employees	7	21	2
Number of machine hours	42,500	–	–
Number of direct labour hours	–	15,000	–

Required

(a) Determine a suitable basis of apportionment for the indirect costs that have not been allocated and prepare a production overhead analysis for Fernando Furniture Ltd.

(b) Calculate the machine hour overhead absorption rate for the machine department.

(c) Calculate the direct labour hour overhead absorption rate for the assembly department.

5. Hannu Ojala OY is a Finnish company that makes two types of skis: the Alpine and the Nordic. The company has two production departments. It also has a canteen, which serves all employees. Next year's budgeted sales and costs for each model are shown in the following table.

	Alpine	Nordic
Selling price per unit	€600	€700
Sales/production volume	2,000 units	2,500 units
Material costs per unit	€80	€50
Direct labour:		
Body workshop (€3 per hour)	50 hours per unit	60 hours per unit
Finishing workshop (€2 per hour)	40 hours per unit	40 hours per unit
Machine hours:		
Body workshop	30 hours per unit	80 hours per unit
Finishing workshop	10 hours per unit	

The production overheads for the cost centres are shown below, together with data used to apportion the overheads.

Production overheads	Total	Body workshop	Finishing workshop	Canteen
	€	€	€	€
Variable costs	350,000	260,000	90,000	0
Fixed costs	880,000	420,000	300,000	160,000
Total	1,230,000	680,000	390,000	160,000
Number of employees	240	150	90	
Floor area (sq metres)	50,000	40,000	10,000	

Required
(a) Recommend a suitable basis of overhead allocation or apportionment for each cost centre, giving reasons for your choice.
(b) Prepare a production overhead analysis.
(c) Calculate an appropriate overhead absorption rate for each production department.
(d) Calculate the predicted production cost for each model.

5

ACTIVITY–BASED COSTING

5.1 OBJECTIVES

This chapter describes activity-based costing (ABC), which offers an alternative to the traditional method of absorption costing. Its name is derived from the fact that indirect costs are first assigned to activities and then to the product or cost unit on the basis of its use of those activities. When you have studied this chapter, you should be able to:
- Explain how activity-based costing can add value to a business.
- Describe the main stages in activity-based costing.
- Calculate product costs using activity based costing.
- Apply activity-based costing to marketing and administration functions.
- Discuss the advantages and disadvantages of activity-based costing.

5.2 NEED FOR AN ALTERNATIVE TO ABSORPTION COSTING

Absorption costing is based on the allocation and apportionment of budgeted (pre-determined) indirect costs to production cost centres and their absorption into the cost of products using an overhead absorption rate (OAR). Each product or cost unit is charged with a fair share of the production and other indirect costs, thus enabling the total cost per unit to be calculated: product direct costs plus indirect costs. Under this system, any overheads that cannot be allocated to a particular production cost centre must be apportioned on whatever is judged to be a fair basis.

Although accountants try to be systematic and rigorous, absorption costing is based on arbitrary decisions about the basis for apportionment and absorption of overheads. In addition, general overheads are spread across the product range with little regard for how the costs are actually generated. Therefore, there is always some concern that the total cost of each product is not calculated accurately. If the business bases its selling prices on inaccurate information, it could have a dramatic impact on financial performance. For example, if the inaccuracies result in selling prices that are too high, the business could lose market share to competitors; if the inaccuracies result in selling prices that are too low, the business will not achieve its planned profit. These problems led to the development of a new approach.

Activity-based costing (ABC) is an alternative to the traditional approach. Its name is derived from the fact that costs are assigned first to activities and then to the cost units on the basis of the use they make of these activities. ABC was proposed by Johnson and Kaplan (1987), who questioned the relevance of traditional management accounting practices to modern business. Management accounting has its roots in the Industrial Revolution of the 19th century, when manufacturing was the major industry. However, as the century progressed, a need for financial accounting began to evolve and Johnson and Kaplan suggest that this split was one of the main causes for what they describe as the fall in the relevance of management accounting. A second reason they give is that modern business is no longer dominated by manufacturing and therefore management accounting techniques based on the needs of manufacturers are not relevant to businesses in non-manufacturing sectors.

> **Activity**
> Due to the increased complexity of production operations, many manufacturers now use computer-controlled operations and robotic methods of production. Why do you think this might encourage firms to consider activity-based costing as an alternative to absorption costing?

The main reason is that advances in technology have increased overhead costs, such as power, maintenance and depreciation of machinery. Therefore, it is critical that these costs are charged to the products as accurately as possible. The increased use of technology has also been associated with a decline in the importance of direct labour and a change in its characteristics. Employees who provide direct labour are often paid on a monthly basis rather than an hourly basis as in the past. In addition, their remuneration is less likely to be linked so closely to the level of production and they are more likely to receive additional benefits, such as pensions and sick pay, which were formerly only given to managers and administrators.

Another factor that is important in some businesses is the amount of inventory held. The correct value placed on *closing inventory* is crucial when calculating the gross profit. Many businesses have moved to just-in-time (JIT) systems, where a low level of inventory is held and the receipts of materials and delivery of finished goods to customers are phased in with the production process. With low levels of inventory, the value of closing inventory has declined in importance.

In addition, increased competition means that businesses are using a variety of techniques to improve the efficiency of their manufacturing operations. These include value-added analysis, which leads to operations that do not add value in converting the materials into the final product being eliminated wherever possible. One of the claims made for ABC is that it enhances the value added to production in businesses with complex manufacturing processes and several different products. This is because ABC recognises that costs are incurred by every activity in the organisation and is based on the principle that the cost units should bear costs according to the activities they use. Like absorption costing, ABC is based on budgeted (predetermined) costs.

Definition

Activity-based costing (ABC) is a system of costing ... that recognizes that costs are incurred by each activity that takes place within an organization and that products (or customers) should bear costs according to the activities they use. Cost drivers are identified, together with the appropriate activity cost pools, which are used to charge cost to products.

An activity cost pool is a collection of indirect costs grouped according to the activity involved.

A cost driver is any factor such as number of units, number of transactions, or duration of transactions that drives the costs arising from a particular activity. When such factors can be clearly identified and measured, they will be used as a basis for allocating costs to cost objects.

Source: Law, 2010, pp. 15 and 117

5.3 MAIN STAGES IN ACTIVITY–BASED COSTING

ABC is based on the assumption that products consume activities and activities consume resources. The main stages in ABC are shown in Figure 5.1. Once the activities that drive the indirect costs have been identified, they are allocated to an *activity cost centre*, which is an identifiable unit of the organisation that performs an operation that uses resources. This allows the indirect costs for each activity to be collected in an *activity cost pool*. Next, the cost drivers are identified and a cost driver rate is determined for each activity cost pool. The cost drivers are then used to charge the

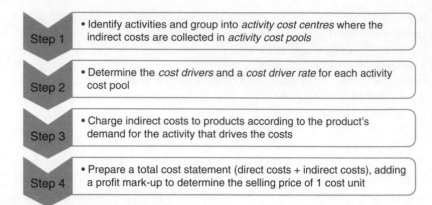

Figure 5.1 Main stages in ABC

indirect costs to the cost units. Finally, a total cost statement is prepared and a profit element is added in order to determine the selling price of the product.

Figure 5.1 makes ABC look misleadingly simple, but each stage involves a substantial amount of research into the firm's operations and costing procedures. This can be highly beneficial, but it can also cause disruption to normal production.

5.4 ACTIVITIES AND COST DRIVERS

In general, the more complex the production process is, the greater the number of activities and cost drivers. A business making a simple product is likely to find that adopting ABC has little impact on overhead costs.

> **Activity**
> List the various activities that the owner of a take-away pizza business has to undertake when making and delivering pizzas to customers.

You will probably have identified some of the following activities, depending on the assumptions you made about the size of the business:

- Recruiting and employing staff.
- Advertising and marketing.
- Ordering ingredients, such as flour, vegetables and cheese (usually referred to as procurement).

- Preparing ingredients and disposing of waste.
- Cooking.
- Cleaning and maintaining ovens and kitchen equipment.
- Receiving orders from customers.
- Delivering orders.
- Dealing with complaints.

With complex production processes and a wide range of products, there are likely to be many activities, but companies usually restrict their analysis to the key activities. Any major activity will probably have several overhead costs associated with it, and these are grouped together to form an activity *cost pool*. The cost pool is then charged to the product using a common *cost driver*.

Activity

Buoys and Gulls Ltd manufactures sailing equipment. The company makes three products (A, B and C). The following information is available for the year.

	Product A	Product B	Product C	Total
Direct material	£95,000	£120,000	£785,000	£1,000,000
Direct labour	£116,000	£145,000	£239,000	£500,000
Numbers of purchase orders	3,000	8,000	89,000	100,000
Number of machine set-ups	12	18	270	300
Number of quality inspection hours	350	180	4,470	5,000
Number of machine hours	6,000	5,500	88,500	100,000
Number of units produced	1,000	2,000	17,000	20,000

The following table shows the predetermined overheads for each activity cost pool and the associated cost drivers. It also shows the predetermined cost driver rate, which is calculated by dividing the overhead by the predetermined cost driver volume.

(Continued)

Activity	Cost driver	Overhead	Cost driver volume	Cost driver rate
		£		
Purchasing	Number of purchase orders	400,000	100,000 orders	£4 per order
Machine setups	Number of machine setups	300,000	300 setups	£1,000 per setup
Quality control	Number of inspection hours	500,000	5,000 hours	£100 per hour
Power	Number of machine hours	250,000	100,000 hours	£2.50 per hour
Total		1,450,000		

As you can see, the business anticipates the annual production overheads will be £1,450,000. You need to remember that this is in addition to the direct costs (direct materials, direct labour and direct expenses). Using the information provided, calculate (a) the production cost per unit for each product and (b) the total production cost for each product and the total production cost for the period.

You can check your calculations against the following solutions.

(a) Cost per unit

	Product A	Product B	Product C
	£	£	£
Direct material	95.00	60.00	46.18
Direct labour	116.00	72.50	14.06
Prime cost	211.00	132.50	60.24
Production overheads			
Purchasing	12.00	16.00	20.94
Machine set-up	12.00	9.00	15.88
Quality control	35.00	9.00	26.29
Power	15.00	6.88	13.01
Production cost per unit	285.00	173.38	136.36

(b) Total production cost

	Product A	Product B	Product C	Total
	£	£	£	£
Direct material	95,000	120,000	785,000	1,000,000
Direct labour	116,000	145,000	239,000	500,000
Prime cost	211,000	265,000	1,024,000	1,500,000
Production overheads				
Purchasing	12,000	32,000	356,000	400,000
Machine set-up	12,000	18,000	270,000	300,000
Quality control	35,000	18,000	447,000	500,000
Power	15,000	13,750	221,250	250,000
Total production cost	285,000	346,750	2,318,250	2,950,000

5.5 MARKETING AND ADMINISTRATIVE OVERHEADS

Businesses that use absorption costing to calculate the total cost of a product tend to concentrate on production costs. Marketing overheads and administrative overheads are often added to the total production cost using a blanket rate for the factory as a whole. This avoids having to determine a separate rate for each production cost centre.

> **Activity**
> What are the advantages and disadvantages in using a blanket rate?

One advantage is that a blanket rate is simple to calculate and apply. The accountant only needs to collect all the overheads together and then select one allocation base. The allocation base is normally related to volume so it could be number of products, direct hour rate or machine hour rate. A blanket rate may be acceptable in a very simple organisation with very few products, but there are disadvantages. The main disadvantage is that, if there is more than one activity, the blanket rate may distort the total cost. For example, if there are two products and the marketing department is spending most of its time in promoting one of them, it would not be equitable to charge the other product at the same overhead rate. Firms using absorption costing will attempt to achieve a better allocation of costs by identifying separate departments and different rates. It will take more time and effort to collect the information and make the calculations, but the resulting costing data will be more informative for management decision making.

In complex organisations, management may decide it is worth the additional costs to implement ABC. In such cases, this cost accounting system can be used to break down the costs involved in marketing and administration by applying the same principles as used for production costs. This enables management to make decisions about the operation of marketing and administration and determine whether it is possible to add value.

We will demonstrate this by applying the principles to Fotobox Ltd, a small printing company that makes calendars using customers' photographs. Each calendar costs £20 to produce and the company adds 15% to cover the cost of marketing, postage and packaging (£20 × 15% = £3.00). However, the owner-manager of the business is concerned that the selling price is not sufficiently competitive and that its customer database contains a substantial amount of out-of-date information. In addition, the accountant has identified the following activities that give rise to costs:

- Printing and distributing leaflets to potential customers.
- Taking orders on-line, by post and by telephone.
- Sending calendars to customers who have ordered them.
- Dealing with complaints from customers.

These activities are shown in the first column of the following table. The second column identifies the cost driver, the third column shows the budgeted (predetermined) annual costs for each activity, and the fourth column gives details of the budgeted driver volume for the year. The final column calculates the cost driver rate by dividing the estimated annual cost of each activity by its estimated driver volume.

Activities	Cost drivers	Cost	Driver volume	Cost driver rate
		£		£
Leaflet design and printing	Customer mailing list	80,000	100,000	0.80
Leaflet dispatch	Customer mailing list	23,000	100,000	0.23
Taking orders	Number of orders	6,000	10,000	0.60
Calendar dispatch	Number sent	4,410	9,800	0.45
Customer complaints	Customer complaints	300	200	1.50
Total cost				3.58

At first glance, the blanket marketing cost of £3.00 per calendar does not look very different from the cost driver rate of £3.58 in the above table. However, the marketing activities cost £3.58 per calendar and this is reducing the predicted profit by 58p per calendar. With the information in the table, management can consider each activity and determine whether savings can be made. For example, instead of sending leaflets to an existing customer mailing list, it may be more effective and less costly to have advertisements on-line and in appropriate magazines. As far as taking orders is concerned, management may decide to accept internet orders only or to outsource the entire operation.

Now you are more familiar with the main stages in ABC, you can compare them with the main stages in absorption costing (see Figure 5.2).

5.6 ADVANTAGES AND DISADVANTAGES OF ABC COMPARED TO ABSORPTION COSTING

If the business already produces costing information that meets its needs, there may be little inducement to undertake the substantial changes required to introduce ABC. Even if the business is not entirely satisfied with its present system, the cost

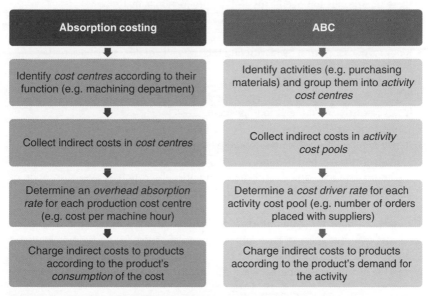

Figure 5.2 Comparison of main stages in absorption costing and ABC

of implementing and managing a new system may be too high to make it worthwhile. Therefore, management needs to conduct a cost/benefit analysis. Unless the expected benefits are greater than the costs, the business should not switch from absorption costing to ABC.

> **Activity**
> What do you consider are the main advantages and disadvantages of ABC compared to absorption costing?

The main advantages relate to the benefit of having more accurate cost information and the disadvantages stem from the costs incurred in acquiring it. You may have identified the following specific advantages and disadvantages.

The main advantages of ABC compared to absorption costing are:

- It provides more comprehensive detail about product costs.
- It generates more specific and reliable data.
- Because it does not distinguish between production overheads and general overheads, it overcomes the problem of finding a meaningful relationship between these non-production overheads and the production activity.
- It provides better information about the costs of activities, thus allowing managers to make better informed decisions.
- It improves cost control by identifying the costs incurred by specific activities.

The main disadvantages of ABC are:

- It can be costly and difficult to implement.
- Trained and experienced staff are required to operate the system.
- It may require substantial investment in IT.
- Managers may not find the information useful.
- It uses predetermined rates and therefore under-absorption or over-absorption of overheads will occur as they do under absorption costing.

The different basis for assigning costs to products is likely to result in a different total cost per unit. This can have important consequences for decision making and strategy in the company. Because the cost information is likely to be more accurate, it could lead to some products being eliminated and changes in the market price of other products. More record keeping will be involved and this may require more trained staff and investment in new computer systems. Installing the system will require teamwork between accounting, production, marketing and other functions in the company.

ABC is probably best suited to businesses operating in highly competitive markets with multiple products requiring complex production processes. In such firms, the arbitrary approach taken by absorption costing does not generate sufficiently specific information to aid internal planning, controlling and decision making.

Information about the use of ABC internationally is relative scarce. There is some evidence that adoption is more widespread in the UK and the USA than elsewhere, with growing use in continental Europe (CIMA, 2009). A survey of 176 large firms in the UK (Al-Omiri and Drury, 2007) found that only 29% had adopted ABC systems and most of these firms were in the financial and commercial sectors. The majority of firms in the manufacturing sector used absorption costing and firms in the retail sector tended to use direct costing. Some of the large firms in the sample did not have any form of costing system, and these tended to be smaller than the others in the sample.

5.7 KEY POINTS

Activity-based costing has emerged as an alternative to absorption costing because of changes in manufacturing operations. The greater use of technology and techniques such as JIT, and the reduction in the use of direct labour has meant that absorption costing fails to provide costing information that is useful to management.

ABC is a costing system in which costs are assigned to activities and then to products based on the product's use of activities. It is based on the assumption that products consume activities and activities consume resources. One of the major problems is identifying the activities that consume resources. This sounds simple, but in reality it is time consuming and complex. Once the activities have been identified and the costs assigned to them, a cost rate is calculated based on the cost driver. ABC offers the advantage of more accurate information than absorption costing because it looks for a closer relationship between overheads and the cause of these indirect costs. However, it suffers from the disadvantage that it is costly to implement and operate.

REVISION QUESTIONS

1. Discuss the reasons why accountants have developed ABC as an alternative to the traditional method of absorption costing for charging overheads to products or services.

2. Describe the four main stages in implementing a system of activity-based costing, defining all terms used.

3. Write a short report discussing the types of business where ABC might be appropriate and the advantages and disadvantages of implementing this type of cost accounting system.

4. Mifone Ltd manufactures two types of mobile phone: the Mifone Personal and the Mifone Plus. The budget for the next financial year is as follows:

	Personal	Plus
Production output	100,000	50,000
	£	£
Direct labour	200,000	100,000
Direct materials	50,000	20,000

The company uses ABC and the indirect overhead costs have been identified with the following three cost drivers.

Cost driver	Cost assigned	Activity level	
	£	Personal	Plus
Number of production runs	150,000	40	10
Quality test performed	40,000	8	12
Deliveries made	20,000	80	20

Required

(a) Calculate the total cost per unit produced for each product.

(b) Prepare a presentation to be given to the board of directors demonstrating the calculations and interpreting the results.

5. Naturelle AG has a factory in France producing two aromatherapy oils: *Bergamot* for the morning and *Lavender* for the evening. The most significant costs incurred by the company relate to the packaging and marketing of the products. The chief

accountant has attended a seminar on ABC and has decided that it would be beneficial to implement it. The following information relates to the production in the current period.

	Bergamot	Lavender
Number of units produced	20,000	4,000
Number of purchasing orders	150	60
Quality inspection hours	1,000	750
Number of batches of materials	2,000	1,000
Cost of direct materials	€35,000	€12,000
Cost of direct labour	€25,000	€16,000

The following table shows the budgeted cost pools and drivers for the year.

Activity	Cost driver	Overhead	Cost driver volume	Cost driver rate
Purchasing	No. of orders placed	€180,000	15,000 orders	€12 per order
Quality control	No. of inspection hours	€50,000	12,500 hours	€4 per hour
Material handling	Batches of materials	€20,000	10,000 hours	€2 per hour

Required
(a) Calculate the production cost per unit for each product.
(b) Discuss the decision of the chief accountant to adopt and implement ABC in the context of the available information.

6
MARGINAL COSTING

6.1 OBJECTIVES

The previous three chapters have described methods in which revenue expenditure is classified as direct or indirect costs. This chapter focuses on a method known as marginal costing, in which costs are classified as variable costs or fixed costs according to their behaviour when activity levels change. When you have studied this chapter, you should be able to:

- Explain the classification of costs by behaviour.
- Construct a marginal cost statement and associated profit statement.
- Conduct breakeven analysis.
- Rank products using contribution analysis.
- Discuss the advantages and disadvantages of marginal costing.

6.2 COST BEHAVIOUR

Marginal costing meets the need for detailed information about production costs in a business where the level of production and/or sales fluctuates. The *marginal cost* is the additional cost incurred from producing one more product or cost unit. Revenue expenditure is classified into *variable costs* or *fixed costs* according to their behaviour when the level of production or sales activity changes. The variable costs per unit are usually regarded as the direct costs plus any variable overheads. Variable costs are assumed to be constant in the short term. Therefore, a characteristic of a variable cost is that it is incurred at a constant rate per unit. For example, the cost of direct materials tends to double if output doubles.

Definition

The marginal cost is the additional cost incurred as a result of the production of one additional unit of production. It usually equates to the direct costs plus the variable overhead costs.

A variable cost is an item of expenditure that, in total, varies directly with the level of activity achieved.

A fixed cost is an item of expenditure that remains unchanged, in total, irrespective of changes in the levels of production or sales.

Source: Law, 2010, pp. 275, 430 and 194

These definitions show that product direct costs are always variable costs, and indirect costs tend to be fixed costs. Some indirect costs can be described as *semi-variable costs* as they contain a variable element and a fixed element. If the separate elements can be identified, the variable element is added to the other variable costs and the fixed element is added to the other fixed costs. For example, the cost of electricity used to power machinery in a factory may consist of a standing charge (the fixed cost) plus a charge per kilowatt used (the variable cost). However, if the separate elements cannot be identified, the whole amount is treated as a fixed cost and added to the other fixed costs.

Activity

Classify the following costs for a manufacturing business into variable and fixed costs:

- Direct materials
- Direct labour
- Factory rent
- Factory manager's salary
- Commission paid to the sales team

Your knowledge of the definitions of variable and fixed costs should have helped you with this activity. Direct materials, direct labour and sales commission are usually classified as variable costs because they change in accordance with the level of production or sales orders. Rent and salaries (unless part of pay is related to productivity levels) are examples of fixed costs.

The following example helps us examine this in more detail. Jimmy Zhou owns a taxi business near London Heathrow called Airport Cars Ltd. The average mileage by a taxi for three months is 15,000 miles and the following table shows the quarterly costs, analysed by nature:

	£
Driver's salary	2,670
Petrol	1,050
Maintenance and repairs	450
Tax and insurance	1,110
Depreciation	870

Jimmy can use this data as the basis for calculating further cost information. For example, he could add up the costs to determine the total costs per quarter for one taxi are £6,150 and then calculate the total cost per mile:

$$\frac{\text{Total costs}}{\text{Total mileage}} = \frac{£6,150}{15,000 \text{ miles}} = 41\text{p per mile}$$

He can then determine the cost per mile for each item of expenditure:

Expense	Cost per quarter	Cost per mile
	£	Pence
Driver's salary	2,670	17.8
Petrol	1,050	7.0
Maintenance and repairs	450	3.0
Tax and insurance	1,110	7.4
Depreciation	870	5.8
Total	6,150	41.0

Although Jimmy now knows the total cost per mile, he may have problems if he tries to use this cost information without understanding the difference between variable and fixed costs. For example, he may want to know what the cost is per mile if the taxi travelled 30,000 miles during the quarter. He may think the cost per mile would remain at 41p, but you may think that it could be lower because the total fixed costs (the cost of the driver's salary, taxation, insurance and depreciation) will remain the same, even though the mileage has doubled. On the other hand, the total variable costs (the cost of petrol and oil) will change in direct proportion to the change in the level of activity. This means that if the mileage doubles (the activity in this example), the variable costs will also double.

Jimmy wants to give a quotation for a contract that will involve driving a customer to the airport every Monday morning and picking him up again on Friday. This will mean driving an additional 500 miles per quarter. This mileage can be done in the driver's current time allowance, so no additional salary will be incurred. Jimmy needs to know the cost of the additional 500 miles per quarter.

Activity

Which of the following figures is the correct cost of the additional 500 miles?

(a)   £205
(b)   £116
(c)   £35

Answer (a) is the result of multiplying the mileage of 500 miles by the total cost per mile of 41p. However, we know that no additional wages for the driver will be incurred, so it would be incorrect to take £205 as the cost of the additional 500 miles. The driver's wages, in this example, can be considered as a fixed cost. In our example, activity is measured in miles.

Answer (b) has been calculated by multiplying the 500 miles by 23.2p; that is, the total cost per mile less the driver's element. But this is not the correct answer to the question, because if you look at the list of costs, you will see that the driver's salary is not the only fixed cost. Certain other costs will not increase because of the additional 500 miles per quarter. Taking them in the order in which they are listed, the costs for petrol and oil will obviously rise with the increased mileage, so they are not fixed. With regard to servicing and repairs, some routine servicing will be carried out regardless of the mileage and this is therefore a fixed cost. However, other servicing and repair costs depend on the mileage. Clearly, tax and insurance are fixed costs and, like the driver's salary, should be excluded from our calculations of the cost for the additional 500 miles. Depreciation, to some extent, is influenced by the amount of mileage, but in a taxi business, depreciation depends mainly on the passage of time.

The above identification of the fixed costs should help you with answer (c). Jimmy needs to identify the total variable costs (petrol and oil) per mile and multiply the result by 500 miles:

$$\frac{£1,050}{15,000} = £0.07 \times 500 \text{ miles} = £35$$

In view of the information available, this is the best answer. If Jimmy wants a more precise answer, we would need to have more details of the semi-variable costs (servicing and repairs) and identify which are fixed and which are variable.

Activity

Circle the correct answer in the following statements:

(a)   If activity increases, total fixed costs will increase/decrease/stay the same.
(b)   If activity increases, the fixed costs per unit will increase/decrease/stay the same.
(c)   If activity decreases, total fixed costs will increase/decrease/stay the same.
(d)   If activity decreases, the fixed costs per unit will increase/decrease/stay the same.

You should have had little difficulty in deciding the answers to (a) and (c) which are drawn straight from the definition. In both cases the total fixed costs stay the same regardless of changes in the level of activity. The answers to (b) and (d) are a little more difficult, but some simple figures may help. We will take as our example a factory where the rent (a fixed cost) is £8,000 per annum. The output of the factory is 1,000 units per annum. Therefore, the cost for rent per unit is £8. If the factory makes 1,500 units one year, what is the rent per unit? The rent cost will still be £8,000, but the cost per unit for rent will decrease to £5.33. Therefore, the answer to (b) is that if activity increases, the fixed cost per unit will decrease. The same reasoning applies to (d): if activity decreases, the fixed cost per unit will increase.

Activity

Circle the correct answer in the following statements:

(a)   If activity increases, total variable costs will increase/decrease/stay the same.
(b)   If activity increases, the variable cost per unit will increase/decrease/stay the same.
(c)   If activity decreases, total variable costs will increase/decrease/stay the same.
(d)   If activity decreases, the variable cost per unit will increase/decrease/stay the same.

You should have found this activity much easier as you have the benefit of the explanations to the previous activity. The answer to (b) and (d) is that if activity increases or decreases, the variable cost per unit will stay the same. The answer to (a) is that when activity increases, the total variable cost will increase, and this means that the answer to (c) is that when activity decreases, the total variable cost decreases.

6.3   CALCULATING CONTRIBUTION

Under marginal costing, only the variable costs are charged to the units. The difference between sales revenue and the variable costs is not the profit, since no allowance has been made for the fixed costs incurred; it is the *contribution* towards fixed costs. Contribution can be calculated for one unit or for any level of sales. The *contribution per unit* is the selling price less the variable costs per unit. The *total contribution* is the contribution per unit multiplied by the number of units sold. Once the total fixed costs are exceeded by the total contribution, the business starts making a profit.

> **Definition**
> Contribution is the additional profit that will be earned by an organization when the breakeven point production has been exceeded. The unit contribution is the difference between the selling price of a product and its marginal cost of production. This is based on the assumption that the marginal cost and the sales value will be constant.
>
> Source: Law, 2010, p. 110

We will now examine this in more detail. Royal Leicester Ltd plans to make a model of Richard III as there has been a surge in the demand for souvenirs due to his re-interment in Leicester Cathedral. The selling price of each model is £2.30. Direct materials cost 60p per unit, direct labour costs are 30p per unit and each model is packed in a presentation box which costs 15p per unit. The total fixed costs are the overheads for the business, which total £850 per week. The normal weekly output is 1,000 units. With this information we can draw up a *marginal cost statement*. The following statement calculates the total contribution and the net profit or loss for the week (assuming 1,000 units are produced and sold).

Royal Leicester Ltd Marginal cost statement for one week	
	1,000 units
	£
Revenue	2,300
Variable costs	
Direct materials (60p × 1,000)	(600)
Direct labour (30p × 1,000)	(300)
Packaging (15p × 1,000)	(150)
	(1,050)
Contribution	1,250
Fixed costs	(850)
Profit for the period	400

The information in a marginal cost statement can be based on predetermined (budgeted) costs or actual costs and it forms the basis of two widely-used techniques for making short-term decisions: breakeven analysis and contribution analysis.

6.4   BREAKEVEN ANALYSIS

Breakeven analysis can be used for short-term decisions such as:

• Setting the minimum selling price of a product, particularly in times when the market is depressed and when introducing new products.
• Setting the minimum level of activity.
• Planning the level of activity to generate a target profit.
• Calculating the margin of safety at a given level of activity.

The purpose of breakeven analysis is to identify the *breakeven point (BEP)*, which is the level of activity at which the organisation makes neither a profit nor a loss. It can be calculated as:

Sales revenue − Variable costs − Fixed costs = 0
or   Sales revenue = Variable costs + Fixed costs
or   Contribution = Fixed costs

> **Definition**
> The breakeven point (BEP) is the level of production, sales volume, percentage of capacity, or sales revenue at which an organization makes neither a profit nor a loss.
>
> Source: Law, 2010, p. 65

The breakeven point can be measured in a number of different ways, which we will illustrate with our example of Royal Leicester Ltd. The following marginal cost statement calculates the contribution per unit, together with the total contribution and the net profit, assuming that the production and sales capacity is 1,000 units for one week.

Royal Leicester Ltd Marginal cost statement for one week		
	1 unit	1,000 units
	£	£
Revenue	2.30	2,300
Variable costs		
Direct materials	(0.60)	(600)
Direct labour	(0.30)	(300)
Packaging	(0.15)	(150)
	(1.05)	(1,050)
Contribution	1.25	1,250
Fixed costs		(850)
Profit for the period		400

The breakeven point can be calculated by applying a formula or constructing a graph. We will apply a formula because it permits a greater degree of accuracy with more complex data. The formula for calculating the breakeven point in terms of the number of units that must be produced and sold is:

$$\text{BEP (units)} = \frac{\text{Fixed costs}}{\text{Contribution per unit}} = \frac{£850}{£1.25} = 680 \text{ units}$$

Once you have found the breakeven point in units, you can use it to calculate the sales revenue at the breakeven point. The formula is:

$$\text{BEP (sales revenue)} = \text{BEP in units} \times \text{Selling price} = 680 \times £2.30 = £1,564$$

Further useful information can be generated by calculating the breakeven point as a percentage of capacity using the formula:

$$\text{BEP (percentage of capacity)} = \frac{\text{BEP in units}}{\text{Capacity in units}} \times 100 = \frac{680}{1,000} \times 100 = 68\%$$

If the business has set a target profit, the level of activity needed to achieve the target profit can be found by using the formula:

$$\text{Level of activity to achieve target profit} = \frac{\text{Fixed costs} + \text{Target profit}}{\text{Contribution per unit}}$$

Supposing the company wants to make a profit of £200 per week, by substituting the figures in the formula, we can calculate how many units must be sold to achieve that target profit:

$$\text{Level of activity to achieve target profit of } £200 = \frac{£850 + £200}{£1.25} = 840 \text{ units}$$

The difference between the level of activity to achieve the target profit (in this case, 840 units) and the breakeven point (in this case, 680 units) is known as the *margin of safety*. This means that the company could miss its target of 840 units by 160 units before it goes below the breakeven point and starts making a loss.

6.5 CONTRIBUTION ANALYSIS

Contribution analysis can be used for short-term decisions such as:

- Evaluating the proposed closure or temporary cessation of part of the business.
- Deciding whether to accept a special contract or order.

- Comparing the cost implications of different methods of manufacture.
- Choosing which of a range of products to make.

The managers at Royal Leicester Ltd want to know the minimum selling price that could be set for the model of Richard III. If you look at the marginal cost statement, you will see that the answer is £1.05, which is the variable cost per unit. Any lower than this amount would mean that the company would not recover the costs incurred in making the model. However, if the selling price was set at this level, the business would not obtain any contribution towards covering the fixed costs.

We will examine this further by looking at another example.

Activity

Cupcakes Ltd makes three flavours of cupcake, which are small iced cakes that were originally baked in teacups. The company shares the fixed overheads equally over the three flavours. A summary of the profit statement for last month is shown below.

Cupcakes Ltd

	Strawberry	Chocolate	Vanilla	Total
Number of units produced	11,200	9,000	6,000	26,200
	£	£	£	£
Sales	5,500	4,500	2,400	12,400
Variable costs	(2,400)	(1,800)	(1,300)	(5,500)
Contribution	3,100	2,700	1,100	6,900
Fixed costs	(2,000)	(2,000)	(2,000)	(6,000)
Profit/(loss) for the period	1,100	700	(900)	900

The sales director has suggested that, because sales of all cupcakes are expected to decrease by 10% next month, production of Vanilla should be stopped until demand picks up. Redraft the above statement (a) showing what will happen if there is a 10% decrease in demand for all flavours, and (b) showing what will happen if the company stops making Vanilla.

Check your answer against the following solution.

Cupcakes Ltd

(a)	Strawberry	Chocolate	Vanilla	Total
Number of units produced	10,080	8,100	5,400	26,200
	£	£	£	£
Sales	4,950	4,050	2,160	11,160
Variable costs	(2,160)	(1,620)	(1,170)	(4,950)
Contribution	2,790	2,430	990	6,210
Fixed costs	(2,000)	(2,000)	(2,000)	(6,000)
Profit/(loss) for the period	790	430	(1,010)	210

The above statement shows the impact of a 10% decrease in sales on profit. It also shows that Vanilla will still make a contribution to fixed costs. However, the revised figures below show that if production of Vanilla is stopped, the net profit will become a net loss.

(b)	£
Contribution	
Strawberry	2,790
Chocolate	2,430
Total contribution	5,220
Fixed costs	(6,000)
Loss for the period	(780)

The difference between the total profit of £210 (£790 + £430 − £1,010 = £210) in statement (a) and the loss of £780 in statement (b) is £990. This is the contribution forgone if the business stops producing Vanilla. The loss of £780 is calculated on the assumption that the fixed costs of £6,000 will stay the same, at least in the short term, regardless of changes in activity such as the cessation of one of the product lines. We can conclude from this that, in general, if a product or service makes a contribution towards fixed costs, it is financially worthwhile to continue producing it. Of course, there may be other reasons for dropping it such as the business deciding to focus its activities in another direction. However in this example, it would be advisable to continue production of Vanilla.

We will now consider another decision the business needs to take. A large hotel has contacted Cupcakes Ltd and offered to place an order for 600 Vanilla cupcakes per month if the price is reduced from 40p to 30p per unit. The order would restore demand, but should the company accept it in view of the low price offered? The general rule is that, if the business has spare production capacity, it is worthwhile accepting a special order, as long as it makes a contribution. The key figures for Vanilla, calculated to the nearest penny, are as follows:

	Per unit		Per unit
	£		£
Current selling price	0.40	Proposed selling price	0.30
Variable costs (£1,300 ÷ 6,000)	(0.22)	Variable costs (unchanged)	(0.22)
Contribution	0.18	Contribution	0.08

As the special price will still give a contribution of 8p, it is worthwhile accepting, but there may be other factors that must be considered before making a final decision, such as the reaction of other customers who may learn of this discounted price.

Now the production manager says he can change the production method so that up to 12,000 Strawberry cupcakes can be produced per month for an additional fixed cost of £500 per month. He estimates that this will save variable costs of 4p per unit. Do you think this plan should be implemented? There is no need to do a full calculation again, but look instead at the maximum possible savings in variable costs and compare them with the fixed costs. The maximum savings will be 4p × 12,000 = £480. Since this is lower than the £500 additional fixed costs incurred, the proposal is not financially worthwhile.

Even when a business occupies a very specialist market, it is unlikely to rely solely on manufacturing a single product, as consumers usually want a choice of products. Therefore, most businesses have more than one product and their managers need cost accounting information to ascertain which is the most profitable. This will allow them to concentrate on making the most profitable product until demand for that product has been met, and then the next most profitable, etc. Marginal costing provides the information needed to rank products in this way.

Activity

So far we have assumed that Royal Leicester Ltd makes only one product, the model of Richard III. Direct materials for this model cost 60p, direct labour 30p, packaging 15p per unit, and it sells for £2.30. The company also makes a model of Henry VII who became king after defeating Richard III at the Battle of Bosworth. Direct materials for the model of Henry VII cost 90p, direct labour 35p

(Continued)

and packaging 20p per unit, and this model has a selling price of £3.00. The fixed costs are £850 per week. Construct a marginal cost statement showing the marginal cost for 1 unit of each model and rank them according to their contribution per unit.

You should have had no difficulty with the first part of this activity if you have remembered the correct format for a marginal cost statement. You do not need to use the information about the fixed costs because they are ignored when calculating the contribution per unit. Compare your answer with the following solution.

	Royal Leicester Ltd	
	Marginal cost statement (1 unit)	
	Richard III	Henry VII
	£	£
Selling price	2.30	3.00
Variable costs		
Direct materials	(0.60)	(0.90)
Direct labour	(0.30)	(0.35)
Packaging	(0.15)	(0.20)
	(1.05)	(1.45)
Contribution per unit	1.25	1.55
Ranking	2nd	1st

When interpreting this information, you need to remember that the reason for constructing a marginal cost statement is to calculate the contribution. If you compare the contribution per unit for each model, you can see that the Henry VII model gives a higher contribution towards covering the fixed costs (£1.55 compared with only £1.25 for the Richard III model). Assuming that it is just as easy to sell the Henry VII model as it is to sell the Richard III model and there are no other constraints, the general rule is that the business should concentrate on making the product that gives the highest contribution in order to cover the fixed costs as quickly as possible and start making a profit.

The disadvantage of ranking products according to the contribution per unit is that differences in sales volume (the number of units sold) are ignored and, hence, differences in sales revenue are ignored. However, we can address this by ranking the products according to the *total contribution*. If 1,000 units of the Richard III model and 700 units of the Henry VII model can be sold in 1 week, the total contribution for each product will be:

Total contribution = Contribution per unit × Number of units sold

	Richard III	Henry VII
Total contribution	£1.25 × 1,000 = £1,250	£1.55 × 700 = £1,085
Ranking	1st	2nd

Ranking by total contribution reverses our earlier opinion and we can now recommend that the business concentrates on selling the Richard III model.

So far we have assumed that there is no constraint on the business from achieving the level of activity required to break even or achieve a target profit. However, this does not reflect business reality, as there is nearly always a *limiting factor*, such as shortages of materials or skilled labour, a restriction on production or sales capacity.

Definition
A limiting factor is a constraint that limits the business from achieving higher levels of performance and profitability.

Source: Collis, Holt and Hussey, 2012, p. 339

The first step is to identify the limiting factor(s) and arrange production so that the contribution per limiting factor is maximised. Perhaps the managers of Royal Leicester Ltd are concerned about the supply of direct materials used in the products as a result of industrial action at the docks where they are imported. This could mean that the company will only be able to make a limited number of products. This presents a dilemma, since the same type of materials is used in both models, but we can see from the marginal cost statement in the previous section that the Henry VII model uses 50% more materials (direct materials are £0.90 per unit compared with £0.60 for the Richard III model). Under these circumstances, which model should the company make to obtain the maximum profit?

When a limiting factor is present, the general rule is to maximise production of the product with the highest *contribution per unit of limiting factor*. We do not know the amount of materials used by each model; if we did, we could calculate the contribution per kilo by dividing the contribution per unit by the number of kilos per unit.

However, we can calculate the contribution for each £1 spent on the limiting factor. The general formula for calculating the contribution per limiting factor is as follows:

$$\text{Contribution per limiting factor} = \frac{\text{Contribution per unit}}{\text{Limiting factor per unit}}$$

Inserting the figures into the formula:

	Richard III	Henry VII
Contribution per limiting factor	$\frac{£1.25}{£0.60} = £2.08$	$\frac{£1.55}{£0.90} = £1.72$
Ranking	1st	2nd

We can now recommend that if there is a shortage of direct materials, management should select the product that gives the greatest contribution for every £1 of direct materials used. This is the model of Richard III, which gives a higher contribution per limiting factor. The analysis shows that for every £1 of direct materials used in producing models of Richard III, the contribution is £2.08 compared with only £1.72 for the Henry VII model.

The following table draws together the results of the three different methods we have used for ranking products, starting with the basic approach and increasing in level of sophistication until we find a method that takes account of factors that place a constraint on the company's profitability.

	Richard III	Henry VII
Contribution per unit	£1.25	£1.55
Ranking	2nd	1st
Total contribution	£1,250	£1,085
Ranking	1st	2nd
Contribution per limiting factor	£2.08	£1.72
Ranking	1st	2nd

The company should reverse its original decision to focus production on the Henry VII model, which was based on the contribution per unit. This is because management needs to take account of the sales volume for each product. We can also recommend that if direct materials are in short supply, the company should still concentrate on producing the Richard III model because it remains the more profitable of the two products.

6.6 ADVANTAGES AND DISADVANTAGES OF MARGINAL COSTING

The advantage of marginal costing over cost accounting methods based on direct and indirect costs is that it recognises that costs behave differently when activity levels change. However, these assumptions about the behaviour of variable and fixed costs rarely hold true over a complete range of activity or for any length of time. The limited range of activity over which the assumptions about the behaviour of costs hold true is known as the *relevant range*, and decisions should be restricted to this range unless investigations are conducted. This leads to a number of disadvantages:

- Marginal costing is based on the assumption that variable costs will vary in direct proportion to changes in the level of activity, but they may also vary for other reasons. For example, variable costs may rise steeply in the early stages because production is not very efficient and rise again at the peak of activity due to pressure of work causing inefficiencies; a special discount on the price of direct materials for a short period may cause variable costs to fluctuate, whilst production levels remain constant.
- Marginal costing is based on the assumption that fixed costs are not affected by changes in the level of activity, but they may change for other reasons. For example, the cost of electricity used to power machines used in the production process may decrease in steps as the level of consumption increases; other fixed costs may increase in steps as additional facilities such as another machine, more factory space, etc. become necessary as activity levels expand.
- Management may find it difficult to identify the variable and fixed elements of cost within semi-variable costs.
- Care must be taken when taking decisions based on contribution, since in the longer term the business will also need to recover the fixed costs.
- Like other cost accounting methods, marginal costing does not take account of non-financial factors that might affect activity levels, such as changes in the motivation, skills and experience of employees.

Definition

The relevant range is the range of levels of activity between which valid conclusions can be drawn from the linear cost functions normally associated with a breakeven analysis. Outside this range it is recognized that the linear relationships between fixed costs, variable costs, and revenue do not apply.

Source: Law, 2010, p. 355

6.7   KEY POINTS

Marginal costing is a cost accounting technique that only takes account of the variable costs of production when calculating the cost per unit. Marginal costing is used as the basis of breakeven analysis and contribution analysis. The principles underpinning marginal costing rest on the assumption that variable costs are not incurred unless production activity takes place, whilst fixed costs are incurred irrespective of the level of activity. However, the assumptions about the behaviour of variable and fixed costs in relation to changes in the level of activity are only reliable in the short term and over the relevant range of activity.

REVISION QUESTIONS

1. Describe the purposes of marginal costing and the importance of contribution.
2. Explain the impact of limiting factors and how you would allow for them. Use a worked example to illustrate your answer.
3. Villiers Engineering Ltd manufactures motorcycles. The company uses absorption costing and has been experiencing falling demand for its products due to a downturn in the economy. Mr Haq, the production manager, is worried because the total cost per unit is increasing, despite strict cost controls. Ms Inman, the marketing manager, is complaining that selling prices will have to be reduced to maintain sales levels. At a recent meeting they found that the selling price suggested by Ms Inman is lower than the total cost per unit calculated by Mr Haq and they concluded that lowering the selling price to increase sales will only lead to even larger losses.

   Required
   Write a report addressed to Mr Haq and Ms Inman explaining:

   (a) Why the total cost per unit increases as production decreases.
   (b) Why marginal costing may be more appropriate than absorption costing for decision making in times of recession.

4. Paddington Ltd manufactures teddy bears. The company's bears are in demand all year round and in the next financial year the sales manager plans to sell 12,000 teddies. The management accountant collects cost information for 1 unit of production (1 teddy bear). Based on last year's figures, each unit will sell for £10 and

the variable costs will consist of direct materials, which will cost £1.00 per unit, and direct labour, which will cost £5.00 per unit. The fixed costs for the year are expected to be £32,000.

Required

You have been asked to provide information that will help the managing director consider the effect on profitability of changes in the level of sales activity next year.

(a) Draw up a marginal cost statement that calculates the contribution per unit.
(b) Draw up a marginal cost statement on the basis that 12,000 units will be sold and calculate the profit or loss for the period.
(c) Briefly explain what is meant by the breakeven point.
(d) Using the contribution per unit you have calculated in (a), calculate the following, showing the formulae in words and your workings:
  (i)   The breakeven point in number of units.
  (ii) The breakeven point in terms of total sales value.
  (iii) The level of sales activity to reach a target profit of £20,000.
  (iv) Calculate the margin of safety in units at the level of sales activity you have computed in (iii).

5. Soundtek Ltd manufactures three types of headphones: Standard, Superior and Deluxe. When planning next year's production, the management team wants to make sure the most profitable mix of products is produced. The following table shows the selling price and variable costs per unit for each model.

	Standard	Superior	Deluxe
	£	£	£
Selling price	100	150	240
Direct materials	30	40	50
Direct labour	30	50	120
Direct expenses	10	25	24

Required

(a) Construct a marginal cost statement that calculates the contribution per unit for each model.

(b) Calculate the contribution per limiting factor for each model on the assumption that the supply of direct materials is limited and rank the products accordingly. In addition, interpret your results by making a brief recommendation on the action management should take regarding prioritising the production of these products.

(c) Calculate the contribution per limiting factor for each model on the assumption that the supply of direct labour is limited and rank them accordingly. In addition, interpret your results by making brief recommendations on the action management should take regarding prioritising the production of these products.

(d) Point out any other relevant matters that management should consider.

7

BUDGETARY CONTROL

7.1 OBJECTIVES

This chapter introduces a major technique known as budgetary control, which generates valuable information about income and expenditure and helps managers with the task of planning and controlling activities, and making decisions to ensure the business achieves its financial objectives. When you have studied this chapter, you should be able to:

- Describe the main stages in budgetary control.
- Differentiate between fixed and flexible budgets.
- Explain the purpose of budgetary control.
- Discuss the requirements for an effective system of budgetary control.
- Discuss the advantages and disadvantages of budgetary control.

7.2 PURPOSE OF BUDGETARY CONTROL

The *purpose of budgetary control* is to help managers to plan and control the use of resources. There are no rules and regulations governing management accounting because the information is intended for internal users. One advantage of this is that management accounting information can be produced about future accounting periods. In the previous chapters on cost accounting, you will have seen that costs are based on budgeted or predetermined figures, which can be compared with the actual figures. However, budgetary control focuses on income as well as expenditure and the need for planning to ensure that the business meets its financial objectives.

We will examine the importance of planning by looking at an example. Splash Ltd manufactures bathroom products. Based on last year's records, the production manager estimates that 15,000 shower units will be needed. He has ordered the materials and they are now stored in the warehouse. The marketing manager has heard that the water companies are introducing a metered system that will allow them to base their charges on the amount of water used at each property. As a result, she has launched a large advertising campaign and believes that 30,000 shower units will be sold. The financial accountant has received a letter from the bank stating that the current overdraft facilities will be withdrawn. Therefore, she has decided to stop any expenditure that is not absolutely necessary. The designer has come up with a new design that incorporates recycling waste water from the shower unit. Trading conditions have been difficult due to a downturn in the economy. The human resources manager thinks that the situation will get worse and has started issuing redundancy notices to the workforce.

This illustrates how a lack of co-ordination and managers following their own ideas can lead to resources not being matched to the demands made on them, and result in inefficiency and waste. This can be avoided if management adopts a system of budgetary control.

Definition

Budgetary control is the process by which financial control is exercised within an organization. Budgets for income and expenditure for each function of the organization are prepared in advance of an accounting period and are then compared with actual performance to establish any variances. Individual function managers are made responsible for the controllable costs within their budgets, and are expected to take remedial action if the adverse variances are regarded as excessive.

Source: Law, 2010, p. 67

A budgetary control system is a communication system that gives information to managers about the objectives of the business and the constraints under which it is operating. Regular monitoring of performance helps keep managers informed of progress towards these objectives. In addition, a formal system of budgetary control allows the organisation to carry out its planning in a systematic and logical manner. By setting plans, the activities of the various functions and departments can be co-ordinated. For example, the production manager can ensure that the correct quantity is manufactured to meet the requirements of the sales team, or the accountant can obtain sufficient funding to make adequate resources available to carry out the task.

By setting separate plans for individual departments and functions, managers are clear about their responsibilities. This allows them to make decisions within their budget responsibilities and avoids the need for every decision to be made at the top level. An organisation is made up of a number of individuals with their own ambitions and goals. The budgetary control process encourages consensus by modifying personal goals and integrating them with the overall objectives of the organisation. Managers can see how their personal aims fit into the overall context and how they might be achieved. By communicating detailed targets to individual managers, motivation is improved. Without a clear sense of direction, managers will become demotivated.

By predicting future events, managers are encouraged to collect all the relevant information, analyse it and make decisions in good time. Control can be achieved by setting a plan of what is to be accomplished over a specified period of time and by managers regularly monitoring their progress. Regular monitoring of actual performance against the original plan permits the identification of any adverse variances (unfavourable difference between the budgeted and actual figures). Not only does this allow managers to assess their performance, but it also gives them timely information that allows them to take any remedial action required.

7.3   MAIN STAGES IN BUDGETARY CONTROL

The first stage in budgetary control is for management to set out their *assumptions* about what is going to happen to the firm's markets and business environment.

> **Activity**
> Make a list of the factors that management should consider when arriving at their assumptions about what is going to happen to their markets and the business environment.

Depending on the type of organisation you are thinking of, the sort of factors you may have included are:

- Changes in the size of the organization's market and its market share.
- Competitors' strategies.
- Changes in interest rates or sources of funding.
- Increases in costs and availability of energy, materials and labour.
- Changes in legislation or social pressures that will affect the organisation.
- The effects of the activities of other related organisations.
- Changes in climate, consumer demographics, social and environmental factors, etc.

Having set out their assumptions, management can then start making predictions about what is likely to happen in the year ahead. However, if they were to leave it at that, they would not be discharging their managerial responsibilities. For example, perhaps they forecast that the business will become insolvent and unable to pay its debts when they fall due. Although this might be an accurate prediction, it would not be acceptable and they must find ways of minimising any threats to the organisation and taking advantage of any opportunities. By setting out their financial strategies and the actions that must be taken in view of their predictions, they are making business plans that will help them meet their financial objectives.

The next step requires detailed plans (the *budgets*) to be drawn up with specific financial plans for each designated part of the business (the *budget centres*), thus covering every aspect of the organisation's activities. A budget centre is typically a department or function in the business. The *budget period* is usually one year and the budget is normally broken down into monthly figures. Initially, it may be expressed in quantitative terms (for example, the numbers of each type of product to be made and the quantity of materials to be ordered), but it will be converted into financial terms for the budgetary control system.

Definitions

A budget is a financial or quantitative statement, prepared prior to a specified accounting period, containing the plans and policies to be pursued during that period. It is used as the basis for budgetary control.

A budget centre is a section or area of an organization under the responsibility of a manager for which budgets are prepared; these budgets are compared with actual performance as part of the budgetary control process.

Source: Law, 2010, p. 67

Responsibility for monitoring and controlling items of income and expenditure is devolved to the managers of the budget centres. The management accounting system provides information to these managers on a regular basis (often monthly) that gives details of the budgeted figures and the actual figures achieved, so that they can compare their performance against the plan and take any actions deemed necessary. The provision of information to all levels of an organisation based on the responsibility of the individual managers is known as *responsibility accounting*.

The next stage involves translating the detailed plans into actions for each manager to pursue.

> ### Activity
>
> Both the production manager and the marketing manager of Splash Ltd need to know how many shower units they plan to sell in the coming year, so they can ensure that the number of shower units to be made will meet the anticipated demand. What suggestions would you make if either of the following circumstances arose?
>
> (a) Many more shower units are made than can be sold.
> (b) Many more orders are received than the number of shower units made.

In situation (a) you may have decided that it is necessary to cut back severely on production. This could lead to redundancies, with machines and other resources not being used to their full capacity. Alternatively, you may have suggested that production continues at the same level and the excess production is stored, which could be very expensive. Finally, you may consider that the organisation should boost sales through price reductions or increased marketing. Both these options could also be very expensive. Although you may think that situation (b) is a good position for the business to be in, it can lead to considerable problems. If the company attempts to boost production, it may need overtime working at a higher wage rate. More machines and larger premises may be required, which may entail taking out a loan to pay for them. If the company fails to meet the orders, customers will become dissatisfied and the firm's reputation will be harmed; customers may go to competitors where the service is better.

Whichever alternative the company chooses, the policy will have to be communicated to all managers. This will ensure that detailed plans can be drawn up which minimise the potential damage to the company's financial performance. However, even if detailed plans are made available to all managers so that activities are co-ordinated, it does not mean that there is control. In any business, managers need to be aware that because the plans are based on predictions, it is very likely that events may occur that prevent the plans from being achieved. For example:

- Prices may rise unexpectedly.
- New competitors may enter the market and offer cheaper products.
- Machines may break down.
- Suppliers may not be able to deliver materials on time.

Once the budget period has commenced, regular financial statements are usually produced comparing actual performance with the budget. This is the final stage, where the individual managers responsible for the budget centres are expected to remedy any controllable adverse *variances* (differences) or revise the plan if necessary.

> **Definition**
> In standard costing and budgetary control, a variance is the difference between the standard or budgetary levels of cost or income for an activity and the actual costs incurred or income achieved.
>
> Source: Law, 2010, p. 430

Assumptions and predictions about what is going to happen to the firm's markets and business environment are normally made at the highest level, following consultation throughout the organisation. Collecting information to measure actual performance is part of the accounting function and accountants are also responsible for issuing financial statements that compare the actual performance with the plan. At this stage, most managers find that they have a role in explaining any variances between the planned and actual figures, and in suggesting the appropriate course to pursue. If there is no formal system of planning and control, there will probably be an informal system. In a very small business, the owner-manager may be responsible for all the stages. In larger businesses, there is likely to be a formal system, with a greater division of responsibility at each stage. Figure 7.1 summarises the main stages in budgetary control.

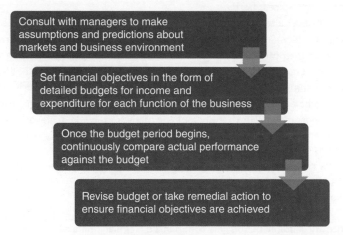

Figure 7.1 Main stages in budgetary control

7.4 BUDGET SETTING

There are two main methods for setting budgets:

- In *incremental budgeting,* management adds a percentage to the current year's income and expenditure to take account of predicted changes in prices. However, this means that the budget will include non-recurring income or expenditure and will not be tailored to the conditions expected to prevail during the forthcoming budget period.
- In *zero-based budgeting,* management starts from zero and builds in each budget figure where it can be justified from the policies and conditions that are likely to exist. This makes the budget much more relevant to the particular conditions expected in the budget period than incremental budgeting.

The budgets give details of the planned income and expenditure during the period that will achieve the given financial objective. In the first instance, the budgets may be measured in quantitative terms, such as the number of cost units to be produced or sold, the quantity of materials required or the number of employees needed. However, they will be converted into financial terms for the budgetary control system. Therefore, both financial budgets and non-financial budgets are normally prepared. Figure 7.2 shows examples of typical budgets for a sales and marketing department (a budget centre).

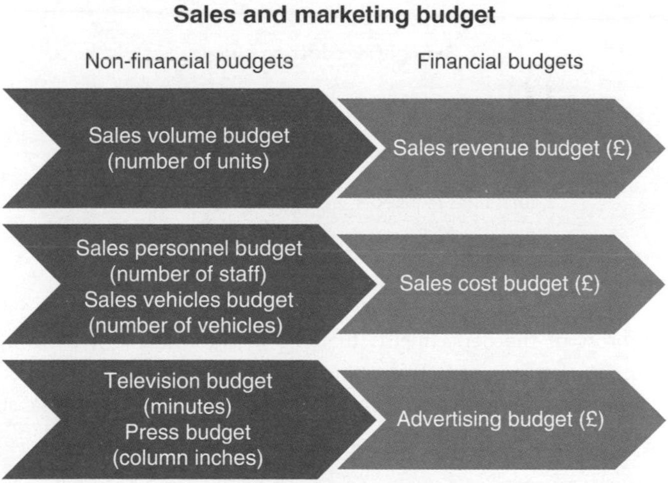

Sales and marketing budget

Figure 7.2 Examples of non-financial and financial budgets

Budgets are drawn up for individual departments and functions, as well as for capital expenditure, inventory and cash flow. Therefore, both functional budgets and non-functional budgets are needed. Non-functional budgets are not the responsibility of a specific functional manager, but require contributions from various managers and the accountant. Non-functional budgets include the capital expenditure budget, which gives details of planned capital expenditure analysed by asset, project, functional area and budget period; the cash flow budget; the budgeted statement of comprehensive income; and the budgeted statement of financial position. The master budget incorporates all the budgets and is the final co-ordinated budget for the period.

We will use an example to illustrate budget setting. Starlight is a solar-powered set of garden lights made by Festive Lights Ltd, which is a small company that only makes this product. We will start with the *sales revenue budget* as this forms the basis of all the other budgets. The company plans to sell 8,500 units of Starlight each year and each unit will have a selling price of £100.

Starlight: Sales revenue budget

8,500 units to be sold × £100 = £850,000 sales revenue

The next stage is to prepare the *production budget*. This budget is expressed in quantity only and is the responsibility of the production manager. The objective is to ensure that production is sufficient to meet sales demand for the period. Like all the figures in budgets, the opening and closing inventory figures are based on estimates.

Starlight: Production budget	
	Units
Sales volume	8,500
Closing inventory	1,870
Total units required	10,370
Opening inventory	(170)
Production volume	10,200

The supervisors of the departments that produce the Starlight then prepare the *direct materials usage budget*. This estimates the direct materials required to meet the production budget. In this case, each Starlight uses 10 units of metal alloy.

Starlight: Direct materials usage budget for metal alloy

10,200 production budget × 10 units of metal alloy = 102,000 units of metal alloy

The next budget is the *direct materials purchase budget*, which is prepared by the purchasing manager to ensure that enough materials are purchased to meet production requirements. The purchase price of metal alloy is £1.50 per unit. As already mentioned, the opening and closing inventory figures are based on estimates.

Starlight: Direct materials purchase budget for metal alloy	
Direct materials usage budget	102,000
Budgeted closing inventory	23,040
Total units of material required	125,040
Opening inventory	(9,600)
Units of material to be purchased	115,440
Total cost (115,440 × £1.50)	£173,160

The *direct labour budget* is prepared by the manager of each production department involved in making the product. The manager needs to estimate the labour hours required to meet the planned production. Each unit of Starlight uses 1½ hours of direct labour and the wage rate is £10 per hour.

Starlight: Direct labour budget for the Assembly Department

10,200 production budget × 1½ hours × £10 = £153,000 direct labour

The *production overhead budgets* are the responsibility of the relevant departmental managers and show the assignment of overheads to each department, as well as indicating whether they are controllable or non-controllable for reporting purposes. The following simple example illustrates the principles. As the title of the budget suggests, in practice it would be factory wide.

Overhead budget for the Production Department (only produces Starlight)	
	£
Controllable overheads	
Indirect materials	30,600
Indirect labour	15,300
Power	5,100
	51,000

(Continued)

Non-controllable overheads	
Depreciation	25,000
Supervision	25,000
Power (fixed proportion)	10,000
Maintenance	11,400
	71,400
Total overheads	122,400
Total labour hours	51,000
Budgeted overhead rate per labour hour	£2.40

In practice, separate *selling and administration budgets* are produced by the managers responsible for sales, distribution and administration. For cost control purposes the budgets for direct labour, material usage and factory overheads are combined into separate *departmental budgets*. For responsibility accounting purposes, these budgets are compared with the actual results at the end of the period to assess how effectively the departmental managers have controlled the expenditure for which they are responsible.

The objective of the *cash budget* is to ensure that sufficient funds will be available throughout the period to cover the level of operations outlined in the various budgets. All budgets are likely to be analysed into monthly or quarterly figures, but the cash budget is likely to be broken down into weekly figures to ensure that any cash surplus or deficit is identified as quickly as possible.

The *budgeted* income *statement* and the *budgeted statement of financial position* are constructed to provide the overall picture of the planned financial performance for the budget period and the predicted financial position at the end of the budget period. These are prepared in accordance with financial accounting requirements but will be based on budgeted information.

When all the functional budgets, the capital budget, the cash flow budget, the budgeted statement of comprehensive income and the budgeted statement of financial position have been prepared, they form the *master budget*. The master budget is submitted by the accountant to the budget committee, together with budgeted profitability, liquidity and gearing ratios. If the figures are acceptable, the budget will be approved.

> **Definition**
> A master budget is the final co-ordinated overall budget for an organization as a whole, which brings together the functional budgets, the capital budget, and the cash flow budget, as well as the budgeted statement of comprehensive income and statement of financial position for the budget period.
>
> Source: Adapted from Law, 2010, p. 277

We will illustrate the interrelationship of budgets by returning to our example of Starlight, which is the product manufactured by Festive Lighting Ltd. The sales director estimates that the following quantities will be sold over the next six months.

	January	February	March	April	May	June
Budgeted sales volume	1,000	1,200	1,400	1,600	1,600	1,700

The production department makes the product in the month preceding the sales and the company has decided to maintain a buffer inventory of at least 200 units each month. On 1 December of the previous year, the opening inventory was 200 units.

> **Activity**
> Calculate the budgeted production volume of Starlight for each month for the six month period January to June.

The best way to tackle this problem is to draw up a table showing all the information provided and then calculate the missing figures.

	December	January	February	March	April	May	June
Opening inventory	200	1,200	1,400	1,600	1,800	1,800	1,900
Production	1,000	1,200	1,400	1,600	1,600	1,700	–
Sales	–	(1,000)	(1,200)	(1,400)	(1,600)	(1,600)	(1,700)
Closing inventory	1,200	1,400	1,600	1,800	1,800	1,900	200

The opening inventory on 1 December is 200 units. To find out how many units must be manufactured in December, you need to consider how many will be needed to cover the sales volume of 1,000 units in January and ensure there is still a buffer inventory of 200 units on 31 December (1,000 + 200 = 1,200). Therefore, the December production volume needs to be the closing inventory less the opening inventory (1,200 − 200 = 1,000). Closing inventory at the end of one month is the opening inventory at the start of the next month. Therefore, the opening inventory on 1 January is 1,200 units. These principles allow you to calculate the budgeted production volumes for the next six months.

Having calculated the number of units that must be produced, the next decision the production manager must take is whether there is sufficient machine capacity and labour to make the product. More machines and labour may be required in the busier months and therefore more space will be required in the factory. If so, all these budgets will be affected. The accountant will want to ensure that the implications of these decisions are shown in the cash budget. It is because of the interrelated nature of budgets that a change in one budget produces a corresponding change in one or more other budgets.

The process of preparing budgets for all the functions and other activities in the business and then drawing up a master budget can take several months. The budgets must be communicated to managers before the start of the budget period. Some organisations adopt a 'top-down' approach, whereby the owners or senior management decide the budgets for each department and function, and these plans are then given to the individual managers to implement. Other organisations use a 'bottom-up' approach to budget setting, whereby the individual managers construct their own budgets and pass them up to the owners or senior managers, who then co-ordinate them into the master budget. Most organisations fall somewhere between these two approaches.

In some organisations, a budget committee is set up, comprising the functional and departmental managers and chaired by the chief executive. The management accountant usually occupies the role of committee secretary, and he or she co-ordinates and assists with the preparation of the budgets using data provided by each manager. The budget committee reviews the budgets submitted by individual managers and ensures that each has the following characteristics:

- Conforms to the policies formulated by the owners or directors.
- Shows how the objectives are going to be achieved, and recognises any constraints under which the organisation will be operating.
- Is realistic.
- Integrates with the other budgets.
- Reflects the responsibilities of the manager concerned.

If a budget does not display all these characteristics, it will need to be revised. This may affect other budgets and there may need to be negotiations between the managers concerned to introduce the necessary budget changes. When the budgets have been approved by the budget committee, they are submitted to the directors for approval prior to the commencement of the budget period. If the directors accept the budgets, they are then adopted by the organisation as a whole and become the working plans for the forthcoming budget period.

7.5 FIXED AND FLEXIBLE BUDGETS

Two types of budget can be set. A *fixed budget* is a budget that is not changed once it has been established, even though there may be changes in the level of activity. It may be revised if the situation so demands, but not merely because the actual activity level differs from the planned level of activity. This can be a considerable disadvantage, because a fixed budget may show an adverse variance on costs which is simply due to an increase in variable costs because activity is higher than anticipated. As you will remember from Chapter 6, this is because total variable costs increase or decrease in proportion to changes in the activity level.

On the other hand, a *flexible budget* is designed to change with the level of activity. Therefore, in a flexible budget, any cost variance can be assumed to be due to an increase or decrease in fixed costs. A flexible budget may be used at the planning stage to illustrate the impact of achieving different activity levels. It can also be used at the control stage at the end of a month to compare the actual results with the planned results.

Definitions

A fixed budget is a budget that does not take into account any circumstances resulting in the actual levels of activity achieved being different from those on which the original budget was based. Consequently, in a fixed budget the budget cost allowances for each cost item are not changed for the variable items.

A flexible budget is a budget that takes into account the fact that values for income and expenditure on some items will change with changing circumstances. Consequently, in a flexible budget the budget cost allowances for each variable cost item will change to allow for the actual levels of activity achieved. A budget that has been adjusted in this way is known as a flexed budget.

Source: Law, 2010, pp. 193 and 195

To illustrate the importance of flexible budgeting, we will return to the example of Starlight. The budget for January is based on a sales volume of 1,000 units with a selling price of £10 per unit. The budgeted variable costs are 75p per unit, the budgeted variable overheads are 25p per unit, and the budgeted fixed overheads for the month are £2,000. At the end of January, the following budget report was prepared that shows the budgeted figures and actual figures for the month when 1,100 units were sold.

Starlight: Budget report for January		
	Fixed budget	Actual
Sales volume	1,000	1,100
	£	£
Sales revenue	10,000	11,000
Variable costs	(750)	(880)
Variable overheads	(250)	(260)
Fixed overheads	(2,000)	(2,000)
Profit for the period	7,000	7,860

The managing director has been sent the above budget statement and is delighted that the actual profit is £860 above the budget.

Activity
Write a brief report to the managing director explaining why he should not be so pleased with the results. Support your report with calculations.

The term 'variable costs' should immediately have alerted you to the problem of comparing the actual results with the original budget when there has been a change in activity level. In this case the number of units sold was 1,100 compared with the planned amount of 1,000. Although the sales manager must be congratulated on achieving higher sales than planned, the company needs to construct a flexible budget to see if they have controlled their variable costs. This is done by multiplying the planned variable costs per unit by the actual level of production.

The variable costs were originally set at £750 for 1,000 units, which is 75p per unit. The variable overheads were originally set at £250 for 1,000 units, which is 25p per unit. If we assume that as the number of units produced increases, the total variable costs increase, the flexible budget compared with the actual results is as follows.

Starlight: Budget report for January		
	Flexible budget	*Actual*
Sales volume	1,100	1,100
	£	£
Sales revenue	11,000	11,000
Variable costs	(825)	(880)
Variable overheads	(275)	(260)
Fixed overheads	(2,000)	(2,000)
Profit for the period	11,900	11,860

Variance analysis involves calculating the differences between the actual and the budgeted figures, investigating the cause of any significant adverse variances and taking steps to remedy them where possible. Actual progress is measured from the beginning of the budget period. At the end of each month, the actual figures for all items of income and expenditure are compared with the plan and reported to the managers responsible. If actual income is higher than the budgeted income, the variance will be favourable. On the other hand, if actual income is lower than budgeted income, there will be an adverse variance. There may also be expenditure variances. If actual costs are lower than the budgeted costs, there will be a favourable variance. However, if actual costs are higher than the budgeted costs, there will be an adverse variance.

Activity
Complete the following budget report by calculating the variances, indicating whether they are favourable or adverse.

Starlight: Budget report for January			
	Fixed budget	*Actual*	*Variance*
	£	£	£
Sales revenue	11,000	11,000	
Variable costs	(825)	(880)	
Variable overheads	(275)	(260)	
Fixed overheads	(2,000)	(2,000)	
Profit for the period	11,900	11,860	

You need to remember that an adverse variance is where actual revenue is lower than planned or actual costs are higher than planned. Compare your answer with the completed budget report below.

Starlight: Budget report for January			
	Fixed budget	Actual	Variance
	£	£	£
Sales revenue	11,000	11,000	0
Variable costs	(825)	(880)	(55) Adverse
Variable overheads	(275)	(260)	(15) Favourable
Fixed overheads	(2,000)	(2,000)	0
Profit for the period	11,900	11,860	(40) Adverse

The budget report shows an overspend on variable costs which needs to be investigated, although variable overheads were lower than planned. The flexible budget shows that the business made a profit of £11,860 in January, but it was in fact £40 lower than planned, not £860 higher than planned, which was the less accurate figure produced by the fixed budget.

7.6   ADVANTAGES AND DISADVANTAGES OF BUDGETARY CONTROL SYSTEMS

There is no single model of a perfect budgetary control system and each organisation needs a system that meets its own particular needs. The following list summarises the main requirements for an effective system of budgetary control:

- A sound and clearly defined organisation with the managers' responsibilities clearly indicated.
- Effective accounting records and procedures which are understood and applied.
- Strong support and the commitment of top managers to the system of budgetary control.
- The education and training of managers in the development, interpretation and use of budgets.
- The revision of the original budgets where circumstances show that amendments are required to make them appropriate and useful.

- The recognition throughout the organisation that budgetary control is a management activity and not an accounting exercise.
- The participation of managers in the budgetary control system.
- An information system that provides data for managers so that they can make realistic predictions.
- The correct integration of budgets and their effective communication to managers
- The setting of reasonable and achievable budgets.

> **Activity**
> When an organisation has a budgetary control system, internal planning and control should be improved, which must be a considerable advantage. What other advantages might there be, and what are the disadvantages of a budgetary control system?

The main *advantages* of budgetary control systems can be summarised as follows:

- *Co-ordination* – All the various functions and activities of the organisation are co-ordinated.
- *Responsibility accounting* – Accounting information is provided to the managers responsible for income and expenditure budgets to allow them to conduct variance analysis.
- *Utilisation of resources* – Capital and effort are used to achieve the financial objectives of the business.
- *Motivation* – Managers are motivated through the use of clearly defined objectives and the monitoring of achievement.
- *Planning* – Planning ahead gives time to take corrective action, since decisions are based on the examination of future problems.
- *Establishing a system of control* – Control is achieved if plans are reviewed regularly against performance.
- *Transfer of authority* – Authority for decisions is devolved to the individual managers.

There are quite a number of problems associated with budgetary control systems. How serious they are depends on the way the system is operated. The main *disadvantages* of budgetary control systems can be summarised as:

- *Set in stone* – Managers may be constrained by the original budget and not take effective and sensible decisions when the circumstances warrant it. For example, they might make no attempt to spend less than maximum or make no attempt to exceed the target income.

- *Time-consuming* – Time spent on setting and controlling budgets may deflect managers from their prime responsibilities of running the business.
- *Unrealistic* – Plans may become unrealistic if fixed budgets are set and the activity level is not as planned. This can lead to poor control.
- *Demotivating* – Managers may become demotivated if budgets are imposed by top management without consultation or if fixed budgets cannot be achieved due to lower levels of activity beyond their control.

The first letter of the above list of advantages and disadvantages of budgetary control form two mnemonics (CRUMPET and STUD) which some students find useful for remembering these points.

7.7 KEY POINTS

Budgetary control involves the preparation of detailed business plans for the forthcoming budget period which are incorporated into a master budget. These plans take the form of budgets for income and expenditure, which are the responsibility of the managers of each budget centre. Financial control is achieved by these managers monitoring the actual performance of the budget centre for which they are responsible against the budget, and taking whatever action is considered necessary to correct any adverse variances within their control.

Zero-based budgeting makes the budgets more relevant to the particular conditions expected during the budget period than incremental budgets. In a business where activity levels fluctuate, flexible budgets rather than fixed budgets provide more accurate information.

REVISION QUESTIONS

1. Describe the main stages in budgetary control and the specific purposes of a system of budgetary control.
2. Discuss the advantages and disadvantages associated with systems of budgetary control.
3. Explain the difference between a fixed budget and a flexible budget, using an example to illustrate your answer.

4. Mr MacDonald owns a farm that produces early crops by growing them in large polythene tunnels. Complete the following budget report for March by calculating the variances and indicating whether they are favourable or adverse.

MacDonald's Farm Ltd
Budget report for March

	Budget	Actual	Variance
	£	£	£
Income			
Strawberries	25,000	24,500	
Blueberries	18,000	17,200	
Raspberries	19,000	19,600	
	62,000	61,300	———
Expenditure			
Salaries	28,400	29,000	
Expenses	12,500	12,000	
Administration	1,800	1,700	
Miscellaneous	700	300	
	43,400	43,000	———
Profit for the period	18,600	18,300	———

5. The managing director of Green and Fair Ltd, which publishes a monthly magazine, has recently introduced a budgetary control system. The accountant drew up budgets for the advertising and editorial departments based on the actual results for the last 3 years. At the end of the first month of the budget period, the actual income was higher than planned, but the actual total advertising department costs were higher than budgeted. The actual costs for the editorial department were the same as those budgeted and the actual profit for the period was higher. On receiving the first month's budget report, the managing director threatened to dismiss the advertising manager for exceeding the budgeted costs. The advertising manager responded by saying that unless the budgetary control system was scrapped, he would resign. The accountant left to join another company.

Required

You work for the firm of consultants that has been asked to advise the company. Prepare a preliminary report covering the following:

(a) An analysis of the problems, and how you think they have arisen.
(b) Guidelines for the operation of a successful and effective budgetary control system.
(c) Recommendations as to what action the managing director of Green and Fair Ltd should take.

8

STANDARD COSTING

8.1 OBJECTIVES

This chapter introduces a system of financial control known as standard costing. In the manufacturing industry, it is closely associated with budgetary control, which was the subject of Chapter 7. When you have studied this chapter, you should be able to:

- Explain the purpose of standard costing.
- Differentiate between ideal, basic, current and attainable standards.
- Calculate the direct materials variances.
- Calculate the direct labour variances.
- Discuss the advantages and disadvantages of standard costing.

8.2 PURPOSE OF STANDARD COSTING

Standard costing is a system for controlling costs in which predetermined standard costs and income for individual products and operations are compared with the actual costs and revenues to identify any variances. Standard costing is mainly used in the manufacturing industry, although it can also be used in the service sector. The main purpose of standard costing is control. This is achieved by comparing the standard costs and income with the actual costs and income. Cost centre managers can be held responsible for investigating any significant adverse variances. Therefore, like budgetary control, standard costing can also play a key part in performance management. The main difference between standard costing and budgetary control is that, while standard costing is applied to products and operations, budgetary control is applied to budget centres and the business as a whole.

> **Definition**
>
> Standard costing is a system of cost ascertainment and control in which prede-termined standard costs and income for products and operations are set and periodically compared with actual costs incurred and income generated in order to establish any variances.
>
> Source: Law, 2010, p. 393

Standards are set in defined working conditions and represent a benchmark of resource usage. They can be set on the following bases:

- *Ideal standards* are based on the best possible working conditions where it is assumed that there are no machine breakdowns, wastage of materials or other factors that might affect production. However, there is some risk that employees will be demotivated by the impossibility of achieving the standards.
- Once set, *basic standards* remain unchanged over a period of years and can be used to show trends in material prices, labour rates and efficiency, and the effect of changing methods. However, there is some risk that employees will feel unchal-lenged and demotivated if the standards become too easy to achieve.
- *Current standards* are based on current working conditions and are appropriate when current working conditions are abnormal. Like basic standards, there is some risk that employees will feel unchallenged and lack the motivation to perform bet-ter than the current standard.
- *Attainable standards* are based on efficient but realistic working conditions where allowances are made for problems such as machine breakdowns, wastage of mate-rials or other factors that might affect production. Attainable standards provide realistic but challenging targets for managers and, not surprisingly, they are the most widely used type of standard.

Standard costs are usually associated with the cost of direct materials, direct labour and other product direct costs. The *standard cost* is the predetermined unit of cost that is calculated from technical specifications. These specify the quantity of materi-als, labour and other elements of cost required, and relate them to the prices and wages that are expected to be in place during the period when the standard cost will be used. It is usual to measure the time in which it is planned to complete a certain volume of work in standard hours or standard minutes. This means that a standard hour is a measure of production output, rather than a measure of time.

> **Activity**
> A company has set 1 standard hour's production at 500 units. In a 7-hour day, 4,000 units are produced. What is this output in standard hours?

To answer this question, you will have needed to make the following calculation:

$$\frac{4{,}000 \text{ units}}{500 \text{ units per standard hour}} = 8 \text{ standard hours' production}$$

8.3 VARIANCE ANALYSIS

Under standard costing, rather than assigning the actual cost of direct materials, direct labour and other product direct costs, the standard cost is assigned. This means that opening inventory and opening cost of sales reflect the standard cost rather than the actual cost of a product. Therefore, there are likely to be differences between the actual costs the business has incurred and the standard costs. As in budgetary control, these differences are known as *variances*.

Variance analysis is the periodic investigation of the factors that have caused the differences between the standard and the actual figures. Financial control is achieved by the individual managers responsible for the cost centres receiving accounting information on a regular basis so that they can monitor actual performance against the standard performance. They must then investigate the cause of any adverse variances that are considered to be excessive and remedy any variances that are within their control. This helps ensure that the business achieves its financial objectives.

> **Definition**
> In standard costing and budgetary control, a variance is the difference between the standard or budgetary levels of cost or income for an activity and the actual costs incurred or income achieved.
>
> Source: Law, 2010, pp. 430–1

Any variances are analysed to reveal their constituent parts, so that sufficient information is available to permit investigation by management. Favourable variances are those which improve the predetermined profit and adverse variances are those which reduce the predetermined profit. We are going to focus on the *direct cost variances*. The total direct costs are known as the prime cost and usually consist of direct materials and direct labour. Therefore, any variance in the total direct costs is likely to be due to differences in one or both of these elements. The *total direct materials variance* can be divided into a usage variance and a price variance. The *total direct labour variance* can be divided into an efficiency variance and a rate variance. This is illustrated in Figure 8.1.

> **Activity**
> In the Stitching Department of Denim Blue Ltd, 100 pockets can be made in 1 standard hour. In an 8-hour day, 950 pockets are produced. Determine whether this will give rise to a favourable or adverse variance.

The first step is to calculate how many pockets should be made in an 8-hour day:

100 units per standard hour × 8 actual hours = 800 standard hours' production

You then need to calculate the variance by subtracting the standard hours' production (800) from the actual production (950) to arrive at a figure of 150. This is a favourable variance because 150 more pockets are produced than the 800 planned.

We need to incorporate this information in the standard costing system, by expressing the variance in financial terms. In a manufacturing business the *direct costs* associated with each cost unit are normally direct materials and direct labour.

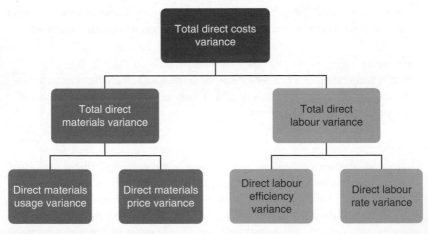

Figure 8.1 Direct cost variances

The reasons for overspending or underspending on either of these costs are based on the following simple concept:

Total cost of direct materials/labour = Quantity used × Unit price

Any variance in the total direct costs will be due to differences in the quantity used, the price per unit or a combination of these factors.

8.4   DIRECT MATERIALS VARIANCE

We will now look at the direct materials variance in more detail. Predetermined standards are set for the usage of direct materials for a given volume of production and the price allowed per unit of direct materials. The standard price is based on the price per unit expected to be paid for the level of purchases projected over the period for which the standard is to be applied. In general, any price variance is considered to be the responsibility of the procurement manager and any variation in the volume or quantity of materials consumed is considered to be the responsibility of the production manager. However, due to the interdependence of price and usage, it may be difficult to assign these responsibilities.

The *direct materials variance* is based on the following formula:

Total cost of direct materials = Quantity used × Price per unit

Standards are set for the quantity of materials to be used for a specific volume of production and the price to be paid per unit of direct materials. The *total direct materials variance* can be calculated using the following formula:

(Standard quantity used × Standard price per unit) − (Actual quantity used × Actual price per unit)

> ### Activity
> Denim Blue Ltd has decided to extend its range to include denim jackets. One jacket requires a standard usage of 3 metres of direct materials which has been set at a standard price of £2.20 per metre. In the period, 80 jackets were made and 260 metres of materials consumed at a cost of £1.95 per metre. Using the formula, calculate the total direct materials variance.

The first stage is to calculate the standard quantity of materials for the actual level of production. As 80 jackets were made and the company planned to use

3 metres of denim per jacket, the standard quantity for that level of production is 240 metres. Inserting the appropriate figures into the formula, the total direct materials variance is:

(240 metres × £2.20) − (260 metres × £1.95) = £528 − £507 = £21 favourable

The difference of £21 between the planned cost and the actual cost is a favourable variance because the company has spent less on materials than planned for that level of production. Although this information is useful, it needs to be more precise to enable management to take any remedial action required. The reason why the actual cost of materials can differ from the planned cost of materials for a given level of production is due to two factors. Either the company has used more or less materials than planned and/or it has paid more or less per unit of materials than planned.

The total direct materials variance can be divided into a usage variance and a price variance, as shown in Figure 8.2.

The *direct materials usage variance* is the difference between the standard quantity specified for the actual production and the actual quantity used at standard price per unit. The formula is:

(Standard quantity × Standard price per unit) − (Actual quantity ×
Standard price per unit)

If data are available, you may find it more convenient to shorten this to:

(Standard quantity − Actual quantity) × Standard price per unit

---

Activity
Calculate the direct materials usage variance from the data for Denim Blue Ltd.

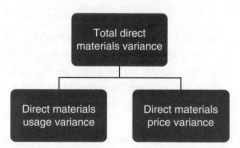

Figure 8.2 Total direct materials variance

Inserting the appropriate figures into the formula, the direct materials usage variance is:

$$(240 \text{ metres} - 260 \text{ metres}) \times £2.20 = (£44.00) \text{ adverse}$$

In this case, there is an adverse variance because the company has used more materials than planned for that level of production.

The final stage is to find out the *direct materials price variance*. This is the difference between the standard and actual purchase price per unit for the actual quantity of materials purchased or used in production. The formula is:

$$(\text{Standard price per unit} \times \text{Actual quantity}) - (\text{Actual price per unit} \times \\ \text{Actual quantity})$$

If data are available, you can use the shortened formula:

$$(\text{Standard price per unit} - \text{Actual price per unit}) \times \text{Actual quantity}$$

> **Activity**
> Calculate the direct materials price variance from the data for Denim Blue Ltd.

Inserting the appropriate figures in the formula, the direct materials price variance is:

$$(£2.20 - £1.95) \times 260 \text{ metres} = £65.00 \text{ favourable}$$

The variance is favourable because the company has paid less for the materials than planned for that level of production. If you deduct the adverse usage variance of £44.00 from the favourable price variance of £65.00 you will find that the total direct materials variance is £21 favourable. Thus, the first two variances explain the third variance.

However, calculating the variances is not the end of the analysis; managers also need to investigate the reasons for the variances and determine whether any corrective action is required. There are a number of reasons for an adverse usage variance. Perhaps inferior materials were used or perhaps the labour force was inexperienced and this led to high levels of wastage. Alternatively, perhaps some materials were lost or stolen. One strong possibility for the price variance is that the company has used lower quality and therefore less expensive materials. This would support one possible reason for the adverse usage variance. Other reasons may be that the business used a different supplier than originally intended or negotiated a special discount.

8.5   DIRECT LABOUR VARIANCES

We will now look at the direct labour variance in more detail, where the same principles are applied. Standards are established for the rate of pay to be paid for the production of particular products and the labour time taken for their production. The standard time taken is expressed in standard hours or standard minutes and becomes the measure of output. By comparing the standard hours allowed and the actual time taken, labour efficiency can be assessed. In practice, standard times are established by work, time and method study techniques.

The *direct labour variance* is based on the formula:

Total labour cost = Hours worked × Rate per hour

The total direct labour variance is calculated by using the formula:

(Standard direct labour hours × Standard rate per hour) −
(Actual direct labour hours × Actual rate per hour)

Activity

The management of Denim Blue Ltd decides that it takes 6 standard hours to make 1 denim jacket and the standard rate paid to labour is £8.00 per hour. The actual production is 900 units and this took 5,100 hours at a rate of £8.30 per hour. Calculate the total direct labour hour variance.

The first stage is to calculate the standard direct labour hours for this level of production:

900 jackets × 6 standard hours = 5,400 standard hours.

The total direct labour hour variance can then be calculated as follows:

(5,400 standard hours × £8.00) − (5,100 actual hours × £8.30)
= £43,200 − £42,330 = £870 favourable

The variance is favourable because the actual total labour cost is less than the planned cost for that level of production.

The total direct labour variance can be divided into an efficiency variance and a rate variance, as shown in Figure 8.3.

The *direct labour efficiency variance* (sometimes referred to as the *labour productivity variance*) is the difference between the actual production achieved, measured

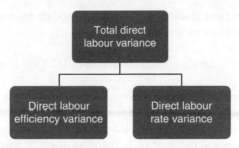

Figure 8.3 Total direct labour variance

in standard hours, and the actual hours worked, valued at the standard labour rate. The formula is:

(Standard hours × Standard rate per hour) − (Actual hours × Standard rate per hour)

If data are available, it may be more convenient to shorten the formula to:

(Standard hours − Actual hours) × Standard rate per hour

Activity
Calculate the direct labour efficiency variance from the data for Denim Blue Ltd.

Inserting the appropriate figures into the formula, the direct labour efficiency variance is:

(5,400 standard hours − 5,100 actual hours) × £8.00 = £2,400 favourable

The *direct labour rate variance* is the difference between the standard and actual direct labour rate per hour for the actual hours worked. The formula is:

(Standard rate per hour × Actual hours) − (Actual rate per hour × Actual hours)

If data are available, you can use the shortened formula:

(Standard rate per hour − Actual rate per hour) × Actual hours

---

Activity
Calculate the direct labour rate variance from the data for Denim Blue Ltd.

Once more, all you need to do is to insert the appropriate figures into the formula and the direct labour rate variance is:

$$(£8.00 - £8.30) \times 5,100 \text{ actual hours} = (£1,530) \text{ adverse}$$

The variance is adverse because employees have been paid more than planned for that level of production. If you deduct the adverse direct labour rate variance of £1,530 from the favourable efficiency variance of £2,400, you arrive at the favourable total direct labour variance of £870. Therefore, the first two variances explain the last one you have calculated.

The most likely reason for the labour rate and efficiency variances is that the company has used more highly skilled labour than originally planned. Therefore, the rate paid was higher and in addition the output was higher than planned. There are other possible reasons, such as the business may have given a pay rise or employees may have had to work overtime and been paid at higher rates. Further investigation would be required to identify the actual reasons and to determine whether any corrective action is required.

8.6   ADVANTAGES AND DISADVANTAGES OF STANDARD COSTING

As with budgetary control, many of the benefits of standard costing are associated with the processes of planning. Standard costing improves financial control and helps managers make decisions, co-ordinate activities and communicate with one another.

Activity
What are the advantages and disadvantages of standard costing?

With your knowledge of budgetary control, you should not have had many problems with this activity. The main *advantages* of standard costing are:

- It improves financial control.
- It establishes a benchmark against which actual costs can be compared.
- It permits a thorough examination of the organisation's production and operations activities.

- As the standards are based on future plans and expectations, the information provided to management is much more accurate than information based on past performance.
- By examining the reasons for any variances between standard and actual costs and between standard and actual income, management only needs to concentrate on exceptions to the planned performance. This improves efficiency.
- Variance analysis may result in cost reductions.

The main *disadvantages* of standard costing are:

- It may be difficult to set standards, particularly in a new or dynamic organisation.
- The standard costing system may be expensive to maintain and the additional record keeping may become a burden to busy managers.
- Standards will naturally become out of date and require revision. In a very dynamic organisation this may happen so quickly that managers lose confidence in the system.
- Information provided by the system is of value only if it is used by managers for control purposes. If the information has no credibility or is not understood, it has no value.

8.7   KEY POINTS

Standard costing is a system for controlling costs in which predetermined standard costs and revenue are compared with the actual costs and revenue to identify any variances. Standard costs are usually associated with the cost of direct materials, direct labour and production overheads. Financial control is achieved by providing information to cost centre managers on a regular basis so that they can conduct variance analysis to monitor actual performance against the standard performance. Timely reporting of variances gives managers an opportunity to remedy any significant adverse variances within their control. This helps ensure that the business achieves its financial objectives.

Standard costing is more commonly used in the manufacturing industry and is closely linked to budgetary control. The main difference between standard costing and budgetary control is that, while standard costing is applied to products and operations, budgetary control is applied to budget centres and the business as a whole.

REVISION QUESTIONS

1. Using the following data, calculate the direct materials price variance and suggest possible reasons for the variance:

   Standard price is £4 per kg
   Standard usage is 5 kgs per unit
   Actual price is £3 per kg
   Actual usage is 5 kg per unit

2. Calculate the direct materials usage variance from the following data and suggest possible reasons for the variance:

   Standard price is £50 per tonne
   Standard usage is 1,000 tonnes
   Actual price is £50 per tonne
   Actual usage is 995 tonnes

3. Green and Innocent Ltd has set the standard price for the direct materials used in its best-selling product at £100 per kg and the company expect to make 4 units from 1 kg of materials. The actual production is 200 units and 52 kg of materials are used at a price of £98 per kg.

   Required
   Calculate all the direct materials variances and discuss the possible reasons for each variance.

4. Speedy & Sons Ltd plans to make 1 unit every 10 hours and the standard rate per hour is set at £9. In a financial period 50 units are made and this takes 460 hours. The total direct labour cost for the period is £5,060.

   Required
   Calculate all the direct labour variances and discuss the possible reasons for each variance.

5. Accord Ltd makes curtains. The company operates a standard costing system for the direct costs. The standard cost of a pair of damask curtains comprises the following elements.

	£
Direct materials (8 sq metres × £4 per sq metre)	32
Direct labour (6 hours × £8)	48
Prime cost per unit	80

The company produced 7,500 units during the period and the actual costs incurred are shown below.

	£
Direct materials (125,000 sq metres)	252,000
Direct labour (91,000 hours)	313,500
Actual prime cost	565,500

Required

Calculate the direct material and direct labour variances. Then use the following pro forma statement to reconcile the standard and actual prime costs for the period.

	£	£
Standard prime cost of actual production		
Direct materials usage variance		
Direct materials price variance		
Direct labour efficiency variance		
Direct labour rate variance		
Prime cost variance		
Actual prime cost of actual production		

REFERENCES

Al-Omiri, M. and Drury, M. (2007) 'A survey of factors influencing the choice of product costing systems in UK organizations', *Management Accounting Research*, 18, pp. 300–424.

BIS (2014a) *Business Population Estimates for the UK and Regions 2014*. Available at: www.bis.gov.uk/analysis/statistics/business-population-estimates (Accessed: 12 March 2015).

BIS (2014b) *Statistical Release,* URN14/92, 26 November. Available at: www.bis.gov.uk/analysis/statistics/business-population-estimates (Accessed: 1 December 2014).

CIMA (2009) *Management Accounting Tools for Today and Tomorrow,* London: Chartered Institute of Management Accountants. Available from: www.cimaglobal.com/Thought-leadership/Research-topics/Recommended-reports/

Collis, J. (2008) *Directors' Views on Accounting and Auditing Requirements for SMEs*, London: BERR. Available from: http://webarchive.nationalarchives.gov.uk/20090609003228/http:/www.berr.gov.uk/files/file50491.pdf (Accessed 12 March 2015).

Collis, J. and Jarvis, R. (2002) 'Financial information and the management of small private companies', *Journal of Small Business and Enterprise Development*, 9(2), pp. 100–10.

Collis, J., Holt, A. and Hussey, R. (2012) *Business Accounting*, 2nd edn, Basingstoke: Palgrave Macmillan.

FRC (2015) *Key Facts and Trends in the Accountancy Profession*, June. Available at: www.frc.org.uk/News-and-Events/FRC-Press/Press/2015/June/FRC-issues-Key-Facts-and-Trends-in-the-Accountancy.aspx (Accessed: 18 June 2015).

IESBA (2013) *Code of Ethics for Professional Accountants,* New York: International Ethics Standards Board for Accountants. Available at: www.ifac.org/sites/default/files/publications/files/2010-handbook-of-the-code-o.pdf (Accessed: 12 March 2015).

Johnson, H.T. and Kaplan, R.S. (1987) *Relevance Lost: The Rise and Fall of Management Accounting*, Boston: Harvard Business School Press.

Law, J. (ed.) (2010) *Dictionary of Accounting,* 4th edn, Oxford: Oxford University Press.

SBS (2004) *Annual Small Business Survey 2003*, URN 04/390, London: Small Business Service.

Waite, M. (2012) *Paperback Oxford English Dictionary*, Oxford: Oxford University Press.

ANSWERS TO REVISION QUESTIONS

Questions requiring a quantitative answer should be set out clearly. Workings should be shown separately. Some questions require a short narrative answer, a brief report or an essay. The language should be formal and all narrative answers should be written in sentences and paragraphs. Where appropriate, the Harvard system of referencing should be used to support assertions. The model answers provided here are taken from the relevant chapters, but students are encouraged to read more widely.

CHAPTER 1 INTRODUCTION TO MANAGEMENT ACCOUNTING

1. Describe how a student can become a qualified professional accountant and explain the need for a code of ethics for professional accountants.

A student wanting to become a professional accountant in the UK must pass a number of rigorous examinations set by one of the recognised accountancy bodies. He or she must then pay an annual subscription to become a member of that body. A qualified accountant can set up in practice as a sole practitioner or with partners, or seek employment in an existing practice. Alternatively, he or she may work as an accountant in the private, public or voluntary sectors.

Professional accountants have a duty to serve the public interest because they are involved in the preparation and auditing of published financial information. They are guided in their work by a code of ethics, which requires them to comply with five fundamental principles (IESBA, 2013, para 100.5):

(a) Integrity – to be straightforward and honest in all professional and business relationships.

(b) Objectivity – to not allow bias, conflict of interest or undue influence of others to override professional judgments.

(c) Professional Competence and Due Care – to maintain professional knowledge and skill at the level required to ensure that a client or employer receives competent professional services based on current developments in practice, legislation and techniques and act diligently and in accordance with applicable technical and professional standards.

(d) Confidentiality – to respect the confidentiality of information acquired as a result of professional and business relationships, and, therefore, not disclose any such information to third parties without proper and specific authority, unless there is a legal or professional right or duty to disclose, nor use the information for the personal advantage of the professional accountant or third parties.

(e) Professional Behavior – to comply with relevant laws and regulations and to avoid any action that discredits the profession.

2. Describe the key elements of the definition of accounting.

In its broadest sense, accounting can be defined as a service provided to those who need financial information. Law (2010, p. 6) is more specific and defines accounting as 'the process of identifying, measuring, recording and communicating economic transactions'.

When identifying the economic transactions, it is important to select the transactions of the business only. This first stage leads to the classification of the transactions into categories, such as purchases, sales revenue and salaries. The economic transactions of the business are measured in monetary terms. This conventional measure is convenient and makes it easier to aggregate, summarise and compare transactions. The transactions are usually recorded in ledger accounts, which are often part of a computerised accounting system, which in turn may be part of an enterprise resource planning system. Communicating economic transactions is achieved by generating a variety of financial statements from the records in the accounting system. These are presented in a format that summarises a particular financial aspect of the business.

3. Compare and contrast the two main branches of accounting.

The two main branches of accounting are financial accounting and management accounting. The purpose of financial accounting is to provide financial information to meet the needs of external users (those not involved in managing the business). On the other hand, the purpose of management accounting is to provide managers with financial and other quantitative information to help them carry out their responsibilities for planning, controlling and decision making. The emphasis is on providing information to internal users that will help the business achieve its financial objectives. Unlike financial accounting, management accounting is not governed by regulations.

Financial accounting is concerned with classifying, measuring and recording the economic transactions of an entity in accordance with established principles, legal requirements and accounting standards. It is primarily concerned with communicating a true and fair view of the financial performance and financial position of an entity to external parties at the end of the accounting period.

On the other hand, management accounting is concerned with collecting and analysing financial and other quantitative information. It is primarily concerned with communicating information to management to help effective performance measurement, planning, controlling and decision making. Therefore, the main differences between the two branches of accounting are that financial accounting is guided by a regulatory framework and focuses on meeting the needs of external users (those not involved in managing the business), and management accounting is unregulated and focuses on meeting the needs of internal users. However, both branches of accounting draw on the same data sources to generate financial information.

4. Explain the advantages and disadvantages of a setting up a one person business as a private limited company rather than a sole proprietorship.

What sole proprietorships and a one person private limited company have in common is that there is only one owner. Unless the owner employs a manager, there is no one with whom to share the responsibility for managing the business and the range of skills available is limited. Both types of business must keep accounting records: the sole proprietorship for taxation purposes only and the private company for taxation and financial reporting purposes.

However, there are some additional differences. The unincorporated status of a sole proprietorship means there are no formalities involved in setting up business and the owner has unlimited liability for any debts or losses incurred by the business. On the other hand, a private company is set up through the formal process of incorporation and thus acquires a legal status that is separate from that of its owner. This gives the owner limited liability for any debts or losses incurred by the company. A further distinction is that the name of a private company must end with 'Limited' or 'Ltd' (or the Welsh equivalent) and shares in the company cannot be offered for sale publicly. Finally, a sole proprietorship has no need to make any financial information public, whereas a private company must publish an annual report and accounts within 9 months of the accounting year end. These disclosures must comply with the Companies Act and accounting standards.

5. Discuss the main differences between a public limited company and a private limited company in the UK, paying particular attention to the financial implications.

Limited companies can be divided into private companies and public companies. A private company is any company that is not a public company. A public company is a company limited by shares or limited by guarantee and having share capital. Most companies are started as a private limited company and, if they are successful and grow large, their owners may decide to re-register them as public companies. They can then obtain a listing on a stock exchange and make an initial public offering (IPO). This allows public companies to raise large amounts of capital to fund their activities. However, it is an offence for a private limited company to offer its shares to the public.

There are two main differences between a private company and a public company. First, a public company must state in its memorandum of association that it is a public company and its name must end with the words 'Public Limited Company' or 'PLC' (or the Welsh equivalent). On the other hand, a private company's name must end with the word 'Limited' or the abbreviation 'Ltd' (or the Welsh equivalent). Second, a public company can advertise its shares for sale to the public and, if it has a listing on a stock exchange, its shares can be traded in the stock market. However, a private limited company's shares can only be offered for sale privately.

CHAPTER 2 NEED FOR COST INFORMATION

1. Explain the purpose of cost accounting and why it is important for managers to have cost information.

The purpose of cost accounting is to ascertain the cost of the designated cost centres and cost units. Cost is the expenditure on goods and services required to carry out the operations of an organisation. A cost unit is 'a unit of production for which the management of an organisation wishes to collect the costs' and a cost centre is the area of an organisation for which costs are collected for the purpose of cost ascertainment, planning, decision making and control' (Law, 2010, pp. 119 and 116). Business is about money and managers need to know the cost of running the business in order to run it successfully. A total cost statement shows the total cost of 1 cost unit (the product direct costs plus a share of the indirect costs). A mark-up can be added to establish the selling price.

2. Describe the main classifications of cost.

Revenue expenditure can be classified by:

- The nature of the cost, such as those that can be identified for materials, labour and expenses, and those for materials that can be divided into the different types of raw materials, maintenance materials, cleaning materials, etc.
- The function of costs, such as production costs, administrative expenses, selling and distribution costs.
- Whether they are product costs, which can be identified with the cost unit and are part of the value of inventory, or period costs, such as selling costs and administrative expenses, which are deducted as expenses in the current period.
- Whether they are direct costs, which can be identified with a specific cost unit, or indirect costs, which cannot be identified with a specific cost unit, although they may be traced directly to a particular cost centre. Indirect costs must be shared by the cost units. Examples of direct costs are the cost of materials used to make a product; the cost of labour if employees are paid according to the number of products made or services provided; the cost of expenses, such as subcontract work. Examples of indirect costs are expenses such as rent and managers' salaries.
- The behaviour of the cost and whether they are variable costs, which in total change in proportion with the level of production activity, or fixed costs, which are not changed by fluctuations in production levels. Direct costs are usually variable and indirect costs are usually fixed. Examples of direct costs that are fixed are patents, licences and copyright relating to a particular product and some direct expenses such as the hire of a particular piece of equipment to produce a specific order.

3. Classify the following costs:

	Production costs	Administrative expenses*	Distribution costs
Factory rent	✓		
Insurance of office buildings		✓	
Electricity for powering machinery	✓		
Electricity for office lighting and heating		✓	

(Continued)

	Production costs	Administrative expenses*	Distribution costs
Tax and insurance of delivery vehicles			✓
Depreciation of factory machinery	✓		
Depreciation of office equipment		✓	
Commission paid to sales team		✓	
Salaries paid to accounts office staff		✓	
Factory manager's salary	✓		
Delivery drivers' salaries			✓
Factory security guards' salaries	✓		
Piecework wages paid to factory operatives	✓		
Salary paid to managing director's secretary		✓	
Salaries paid to factory canteen staff	✓		
Fees paid to advertising agency		✓	
Maintenance of machinery	✓		
Accounting software		✓	
Bonuses for factory staff	✓		
Training course for clerical staff		✓	

*Includes selling costs

4. Portland Paving Ltd

(a)

Total cost (2,000 units)

	£
Direct costs	
Direct materials (6,000 + 200)	6,200
Direct labour	10,000
Prime cost	16,200
Production overheads (1,000 + 2,000 + 700 + 1,500 + 2,500 + 2,200 + 800 + 900)	11,600
Production cost	27,800

Administrative expenses (400 + 800 + 200 + 1, 800 +
2,200 + 1,600)   7,000
Distribution overheads (500 + 800)   1,300
Total cost   36,100

(b) Interpretation
Should demonstrate awareness that total cost is built from a number of key
elements and should explain the terms used.

5. **Portland Paving Ltd**

Total cost (1 unit)*

	£
Direct costs	
Direct materials	3.10
Direct labour	5.00
Prime cost	8.10
Production overheads	5.80
Production cost	13.90
Indirect costs	
Administrative expenses	3.50
Distribution overheads	0.65
Total cost	18.05
Profit (Production cost £13.90 × 50%)	6.95
Selling price	25.00

*The workings are the same as in question 4(a), but divided by 2,000.

CHAPTER 3 COSTING FOR PRODUCT DIRECT COSTS

1. Describe the main stages in controlling direct materials.

In a manufacturing business the control of materials used in the production process
is essential to ensure that production is not delayed due to shortages and that the

business does not tie up capital by storing excess quantities of inventory. The main stages in material control are:

- The stores or production department sends a *purchase requisition* to the purchasing department, giving details of the quantity and type of materials required.
- The buyer in the purchasing department sends a *purchase order* to the supplier.
- The supplier sends the materials with a *goods received note*, which is checked against the materials received and the purchase order.
- The materials are added to the existing inventory in the stores and the quantity is added to the inventory level shown on the *bin card*.
- When materials are required, the production department sends a *materials requisition* to the stores and the stores issues the materials and deducts the quantity from the inventory level shown on the *bin card*. Periodic stocktaking ensures that a physical count of all inventories is made to confirm that the actual quantities support the levels shown on the bin cards.

In a well-managed business, materials are available in the right place, at the right time and in the right quantities, and all materials are properly accounted for.

2. Compare and contrast the advantages and disadvantages of the FIFO and CWA methods.

The main advantage of the FIFO cost method is that it is acceptable to financial accountants in the UK and to HM Revenue and Customs, which means that not only can it be used for management accounting purposes, but also for financial reporting and taxation purposes. However, this advantage also applies to the CWA cost method. The FIFO method is the logical choice if it coincides with the order in which inventory is physically issued to production (for example materials with a finite life where it makes sense to issue those that have been stored the longest first). However, the CWA is the logical choice if inventory consists of volume and liquid materials where an averaging method makes sense because it may not be possible to differentiate between old and new inventory stored in bulk containers.

While the FIFO has the benefit of charging the cost of direct materials against profits in the same order as costs are incurred, the CWA offers the advantage of smoothing out the impact of price changes in the statement of comprehensive income. However, the FIFO method is complex and an arithmetical burden, even when a spreadsheet is used. While the cost of direct materials issued to production is based on historical prices, the value of inventory at end of period is close to current prices. On the other hand, the CWA method requires the prices of materials issued to production to be recalculated every time a new consignment is received, which can be done relatively easily by entering the quantity and pricing information from the source documents into a spreadsheet or specialist software package. The CWA method also offers the advantage that it takes account of quantities purchased and changing prices, including prices relating to previous periods. Nevertheless, the prices of materials issued may not match any of the prices actually paid and the value of closing inventory will lag behind current prices if prices are rising

3. Monica's wages are based on piecework and she is paid £5 per piecework hour. Calculate her pay for a 36-hour week in which she produces the following units:

Product	Number of units	Time allowance per unit	Total piecework hours
A	12	0.8 hours	9.6
B	30	0.6 hours	18.0
C	24	0.5 hours	12.0
			39.6
		Pay (39.6 hours × £10)	£396

4. Butler Ltd

(a)

(i) FIFO	Receipts			Issues			Inventory balance	
Dec	Quantity	Price	Value	Quantity	Price	Value	Quantity	Value
	kg	£	£	kg	£	£	kg	£
1							500	1,000.00
2				450	2.00	900.00	50	100.00
7	550	2.10	1,155				600	1,255.00
8				50	2.00	100.00	550	1,155.00
8				450	2.10	945.00	100	210.00
14	600	2.20	1,320				700	1,530.00
15				100	2.10	210.00	600	1,320.00
15				500	2.20	1,100.00	100	220.00

(Continued)

30	500	2.30	1,150				600	1,370.00
31				100	2.20	220.00	500	1,150.00
Total			3,625			3,475.00		

Interpretation: Under FIFO, the cost of metal alloy issued to production during December was £3,475. At the end of the month, the quantity of closing inventory was 500 kg valued at £1,150.

(ii) AVCO	Receipts			Issues			Inventory balance	
Dec	Quantity	Price	Value	Quantity	Price	Value	Quantity	Value
	kg	£	£	kg	£	£	kg	£
1							500	1,000.00
2				450	2.00	900.00	50	100.00
7	550	2.10	1,155				600	1,255.00
8				500	2.09	1,045.83	100	209.17
14	600	2.20	1,320				700	1,529.17
15				600	2.18	1,310.71	100	218.45
30	500	2.30	1,150				600	1,368.45
31				100	2.28	228.08	500	1,140.38
Total			3,625			3,484.62		

Interpretation: Under AVCO, the cost of metal alloy issued to production during December was £3,484.62. At the end of the month, the quantity of closing inventory was 500 kg valued at £1,140.38.

(b) Discuss the advantages and disadvantages of the two methods and conclude by recommending which method Butler Ltd should adopt, giving at least five reasons.

The answer should compare and contrast the advantages and disadvantages of the FIFO and AVCO. It should conclude with a recommendation based on at least five benefits of the chosen method.

5. Sergio Sauces Ltd

(a)

(i) FIFO	Receipts			Issues			Inventory balance	
Sept	Quantity	Price	Value	Quantity	Price	Value	Quantity	Value
	tonne	£	£	tonne	£	£	tonne	£
1	1,000	5.00	5,000				1,000	5,000.00
2	1,000	5.50	5,500				2,000	10,500.00
3				750	5.00	3,750.00	1,250	6,750.00
14				250	5.00	1,250.00	1,000	5,500.00
				500	5.50	2,750.00	500	2,750.00
15	1,000	6.00	6,000				1,500	8,750.00
16				500	5.50	2,750.00	1,000	6,000.00
				250	6.00	1,500.00	750	4,500.00
29	1,000	6.50	6,500				1,750	11,000.00
30				750	6.00	4,500.00	1,000	6,500.00
Total			23,000			16,500.00		

Interpretation: Under FIFO, the cost of tomatoes issued to production during September was £16,500. At the end of the month, the quantity of closing inventory was 1,000 kg valued at £6,500.

(ii) AVCO	Receipts			Issues			Inventory balance	
Sept	Quantity	Price	Value	Quantity	Price	Value	Quantity	Value
	tonnes	£	£	tonnes	£	£	tonnes	£
1	1,000	5.00	5,000				1,000	5,000.00
2	1,000	5.50	5,500				2,000	10,500.00
3				750	5.25	3,937.50	1,250	6,562.50
14				750	5.25	3,937.50	500	2,625.00
15	1,000	6.00	6,000				1,500	8,625.00

(Continued)

(ii) AVCO	Receipts			Issues			Inventory balance	
16				750	5.75	4,312.50	750	4,312.50
29	1,000	6.50	6,500				1,750	10,812.50
30				750	6.18	4,633.93	1,000	6,178.57
Total			23,000			16,821.43		

Interpretation: Under AVCO, the cost of tomatoes issued to production during September was £16,821.43. At the end of the month, the quantity of closing inventory was 1,000 kg valued at £6,178.57.

(b) Identify which of the two methods would give the higher profit for the month in this particular case, giving your reasons.

The basic argument is that the higher the value of closing inventory, the higher the profit. Costs reduce revenue and closing inventory reduces the cost of sales for the period. Reference should be made to the fact that when prices are rising, the value of closing inventory under the FIFO method is higher than under the CWA method. Under the FIFO cost method, the valuation is closer to current prices, whereas under the CWA method price increases are smoothed out and the value of closing inventory lags behind the current price. Therefore, the FIFO cost method gives the higher profit under these circumstances.

CHAPTER 4 ABSORPTION COSTING

1. Describe the main stages for calculating the total cost per unit under an absorption costing system.

'Absorption costing is the cost accounting system in which the overheads of an organization are charged to the production by means of the process of absorption. Costs are first allocated or apportioned to the cost centres, where they are absorbed into the cost unit using absorption rates' (Law, 2010, p. 2). There are four main stages as follows:

- Collect indirect costs in cost centres on the basis of allocation or apportionment.
- Determine an overhead absorption rate (OAR) for each production cost centre (for example cost per direct labour hour).

- Charge indirect costs to products using the OAR and a measure of the product's consumption of the cost centre's cost (for example number of direct labour hours).
- Calculate the cost per unit.

2. Explain what it means to allocate, apportion and absorb indirect costs.

In some cases, indirect costs that have been classified by nature can be wholly identified with one particular cost centre (for example wages and depreciation on machinery relating to a particular production department that has been designated as a cost centre). These overheads can simply be allocated to that cost centre (for example the whole amount of the annual allowance for depreciation on machinery in that department is allocated to that cost centre). However, indirect costs that are associated with more than one cost centre must be apportioned over the cost centres benefiting from them (for example factory rent could be apportioned over the production cost centres on the basis of the proportion of space each department occupies in the factory).

An overhead absorption rate is calculated in advance of an accounting period and used to charge the indirect costs to the production for that period (Law, 2010). The choice of absorption rate depends on the basis of apportionment and the resources used. The main rates used are:

- The cost unit overhead absorption rate.
- The direct labour hour overhead absorption rate.
- The machine hour overhead absorption rate.

3. Discuss the advantages and disadvantages of using an absorption costing system for calculating the total cost of a product.

The advantages of absorption costing are that it provides a means of sharing the total overheads of a business in the manufacturing sector over the various production cost centres and the overheads for a particular production cost centre over the various products passing through it. It allows production overheads to be allocated or apportioned to the cost centres on a fair basis and absorbed into the cost unit using an appropriate overhead absorption rate. Non-production overheads are absorbed into the cost unit by adding a percentage based on the proportion of non-production overheads to the total production cost.

However, there are a number of disadvantages. Not only is this cost accounting system unsuitable for businesses in the service sector, but a major limitation of absorption costing is that it is based on arbitrary decisions about the basis for apportioning and absorbing the overheads. Normally predetermined overhead absorption rates are used because the actual figures are not available until the end of the period, but if the predetermined overhead that has been absorbed is higher than the actual overhead, it will result in over-absorption, which reduces expenses in the statement of comprehensive income. On the other hand, if the predetermined overhead that has been absorbed is lower than the actual overhead, it will result in under-absorption, which increases expenses in the statement of comprehensive income. In addition, general overheads are spread across the product range with little regard for how the costs are actually generated. Therefore, there is always some concern that the total cost of each product is not being calculated in the most precise manner. If the business is miscalculating the cost of its products and basing its selling prices on this inaccurate information, it could have a dramatic impact on financial performance. For example, if the inaccuracies result in selling prices that are too high, the business could lose market share to competitors; if they result in selling prices that are too low, the business will not achieve its planned profit.

A further criticism of absorption costing is that it assigns indirect costs in proportion to the number of units produced (volume), but many resources used in support activities are not related to volume (for example machine set-up, where the cost varies with the complexity of the production process and the diversity of the product range). This means too large a proportion of the cost of support activities is assigned to high volume products that cause little diversity, and too small a proportion is assigned to low volume products that use more support activities.

4. Fernando Garden Furniture Ltd

(a)

Production overhead analysis

Overhead	Total	Basis of apportionment	Machine department	Assembly department	Maintenance department
	£		£	£	£
Indirect materials	24,500	Allocated	12,000	10,000	2,500
Indirect labour	54,500	Allocated	14,000	18,000	22,500
Rent and rates	26,000	Area	13,000	10,400	2,600
Electricity	4,000	Area	2,000	1,600	400

Overhead	Total	Basis of apportionment	Machine department	Assembly department	Maintenance department
	£		£	£	£
Depreciation of machinery	36,000	Value of machinery	24,000	8,000	4,000
Supervisors' salaries	42,000	No. of employees	9,800	29,400	2,800
Subtotal	187,000		74,800	77,400	34,800
Apportioned service costs	–	Value of machinery	26,100	8,700	(34,800)
Total	187,000		100,900	86,100	–

(b) Machine department OAR

$$\frac{\text{Cost centre overheads}}{\text{No. of machine hours}} = \frac{£100,900}{42,500} = £2.37 \text{ per machine hour}$$

(c) Assembly department OAR

$$\frac{\text{Cost centre overheads}}{\text{Direct labour hours}} = \frac{£86,100}{15,000} = £5.74 \text{ per direct labour hour}$$

5. Hannu Ojala OY

(a)

Production overhead analysis

	Basis of apportionment*	Body workshop	Finishing workshop	Canteen	Total
		€	€	€	€
Production overheads	Allocated	680,000	390,000	160,000	1,230,000
Apportioned service costs	Number of employees	100,000	60,000		
Total		780,000	450,000		

*Students should give a rationale for the basis of apportionment used.

(b) Overhead absorption rates

Body workshop: Total machine hours $(30 \times 2,000) + (80 \times 2,500) = 260,000$

$$\frac{\text{Cost centre overheads}}{\text{No. of machine hours}} = \frac{€780,000}{260,000} = €3.00 \text{ per unit}$$

Finishing workshop:

Total direct labour hours $(40 \times 2,000) + (40 \times 2,500) = 180,000$

$$\frac{\text{Cost centre overheads}}{\text{No. of direct labour hours}} = \frac{€450,000}{180,000} = €2.50 \text{ per unit}$$

(c) Predicted production cost per unit

	Alpine		Nordic	
	€		€	
Direct costs				
Direct materials (given)	80		50	
Direct labour (hours × pay rate)				
Body workshop	150	(50 hrs × £3)	180	(60 hrs × £3)
Finishing workshop	80	(40 hrs × £2)	80	(40 hrs × £2)
Prime cost	310		310	
Indirect costs				
Body workshop (Machine hours)	90	(30 hrs × £3)	240	(80 hrs × £3)
Finishing workshop (Direct labour hours)	100	(40 hrs × £2.50)	100	(40 hrs × £2.50)
Production cost	500		650	

CHAPTER 5 ACTIVITY–BASED COSTING

1. Discuss the reasons why accountants have developed ABC as an alternative to the traditional method of absorption costing for charging overheads to products or services.

One of the main criticisms of absorption costing is that this cost accounting system is based on arbitrary decisions about the basis for apportionment and absorption of overheads. In addition, general overheads are spread across the product range with little regard for how the costs are actually generated. Therefore, there is always some concern that the total cost of each product is not being calculated in the most precise way. If a business is miscalculating the cost of its products and basing its selling prices on this inaccurate information, it could have a dramatic impact on financial performance. For example, if the inaccuracies result in selling prices that are too high, the business could lose market share to its competitors; if they result in selling prices that are too low, the business will not achieve its planned profit.

Absorption costing was developed at a time when the majority of firms were in the manufacturing sector and tended to carry high levels of inventory. Therefore, the valuation of inventory was very important. In addition, direct labour was a major element in the cost of a product and overheads were relatively small, so inaccuracies in apportioning indirect costs to cost units did not have a significant effect on the total cost, which is calculated to determine the selling price or to value closing inventory. Today, advanced manufacturing technology (for example computer-controlled processes and robotics) has decreased direct labour costs and increased overheads (for example power, maintenance and depreciation on machinery and equipment). Moreover, just-in-time techniques mean little or no inventory is held.

Activity-based costing (ABC) was proposed by Johnson and Kaplan (1987), who questioned the relevance of traditional management accounting practices to modern business. The increased importance of financial accounting as one of the main branches of accounting and the fact that the majority of firms are now in the service sector mean that traditional management accounting techniques based on the needs of manufacturers are irrelevant to many businesses today. ABC is 'a system of costing ... that recognizes that costs are incurred by each activity that takes place within an organization and that products (or customers) should bear costs according to the activities they use. Cost drivers are identified, together with the appropriate activity cost pools, which are used to charge cost to products' (Law, 2010, p. 15). The main assumption is that products (goods or services) consume activities and activities consume resources. This overcomes the problem of finding a meaningful relationship between non-production overheads and the production activity.

2. Describe the four main stages in implementing a system of activity-based costing, defining all terms used.

Activity-based costing (ABC) is a system of costing 'that recognizes that costs are incurred by each activity that takes place within an organization and that products (or customers) should bear costs according to the activities they use. Cost drivers are identified, together with the appropriate activity cost pools, which are used to charge cost to products … An activity cost pool is a collection of indirect costs grouped according to the activity involved' (Law, 2010, p. 15). The implementation of an activity-based costing system involves four main steps:

- Identify the main activities in the organisation and classify them into activity centres if there are a large number of different activities. An activity centre is an identifiable unit of the organisation that performs an operation that uses resources. For most organisations the first activity will be the purchase of materials. This will involve several sub-activities, such as drawing up material specifications, selecting suppliers, placing the order, receiving and inspecting the materials that have been delivered.
- Identify the cost drivers associated with each activity centre. A cost driver is 'any factor such as number of units, number of transactions, or duration of transactions that drives the costs arising from a particular activity. When such factors can be clearly identified and measured, they will be used as a basis for allocating costs to cost objects' (Law, 2010, p. 117). For example, a cost driver for the purchase of materials would be the number of orders placed; for customer support, it might be the number of calls answered; for a quality control activity, it might be the number of hours of inspection conducted. Some activities have multiple cost drivers.
- Calculate the cost driver rate, which is the cost per unit of activity. For example, in purchasing it would be the cost per order placed.
- Assign costs to the products by multiplying the cost driver rate by the volume of the cost driver units consumed by the product. With purchasing, the cost driver rate will be calculated on the basis of orders placed. For example, if Product A requires 15 orders to be placed in January, the cost of purchasing activity for Product A will be 15 times the cost driver rate.

3. Write a short report discussing the types of business where ABC might be appropriate and the advantages and disadvantages of implementing this type of cost accounting system.

Activity-based costing is best suited to businesses that operate in highly competitive markets and which have many different products that require complex production processes. In such firms the arbitrary process of absorption costing does not generate sufficiently specific information to aid managers in planning, controlling and decision making.

The main advantages of activity-based costing are:

- It provides more comprehensive detail about product costs.
- It generates data that is more specific and reliable than traditional costing.
- Because it does not distinguish between production overheads and general overheads, it overcomes the problem of finding a meaningful relationship between these non-production overheads and the production activity.
- It provides better information about the costs of activities, thus allowing managers to make more informed decisions.
- It improves cost control by identifying the costs incurred by specific activities.

The main disadvantages are:

- It can be costly and difficult to implement.
- Trained and experienced staff are required to operate the system.
- Substantial IT costs may be required.
- Managers may not find the information useful.
- It uses predetermined rates and therefore under-absorption or over-absorption of overheads will still occur as they do under absorption costing.

Managers should be aware that the different basis for assigning costs to products is likely to result in a different total cost per unit. This can have important consequences for decision making and strategy in the company. More accurate cost information could lead to some products being eliminated and changes in the market price of other products. Installing the system will require teamwork between accounting, production, marketing and other functions in the company. Therefore, management should conduct a cost/benefit analysis before implementing activity-based costing and, unless the expected benefits are greater than the costs, the firm should not move from absorption costing.

4. Mifone Ltd

(a)

	Rate	Personal	Plus	Total
	£	£	£	£
Direct costs				
Direct labour		200,000	100,000	300,000
Direct materials		50,000	20,000	70,000

(Continued)

	Rate	Personal	Plus	Total
Indirect costs				
Production	3,000	120,000	30,000	150,000
Quality	2,000	16,000	24,000	40,000
Delivery	200	16,000	4,000	20,000
Total cost		402,000	178,000	580,000
Divide by number of units produced		100,000	50,000	
Cost per unit		4.02	3.56	

(b) The above calculations should be incorporated in the presentation for the board of directors together with a clear interpretation.

5. Naturelle AG

(a)

	Bergamot	Lavender
	€	€
Direct costs		
Direct materials	35,000	12,000
Direct labour	25,000	16,000
Indirect overhead costs		
Purchasing	1,800	720
Quality control	4,000	3,000
Material handling	4,000	2,000
Production cost	69,800	33,720
Divide by units produced	20,000	4,000
Production cost per unit	€3.49	€8.43

(b) This seems to be a simple production process with little use of technology. Therefore, it is not the type of operation that one would usually recommend adopts activity-based costing. The overhead costs are modest compared to the cost of direct materials and direct labour and the company would be better advised to concentrate on controlling their direct costs. No information is given on the packaging costs, and the advertising and it would be worthwhile identifying these costs. A fairly simple absorption costing system may be a better approach for this company.

CHAPTER 6 MARGINAL COSTING

1. Describe the purposes of marginal costing and the importance of contribution.

The purpose of marginal costing is to meet the need for detailed information about costs in a business where production levels fluctuate. It requires revenue expenditure to be classified into variable costs or fixed costs according to the behaviour of the cost when the level of production or sales activity changes. A variable cost is 'an item of expenditure that, in total, varies directly with the level of activity achieved' and a fixed cost is 'an item of expenditure that remains unchanged, in total, irrespective of changes in the levels of production or sales' (Law, 2010, pp. 430 and 194). The variable costs per unit are usually regarded as the direct costs plus any variable overheads and are assumed to be constant in the short term. Therefore, a characteristic of a variable cost is that it is incurred at a constant rate per unit; for example, the cost of direct materials will tend to double if output doubles. Semi-variable costs contain both variable and fixed elements and must be analysed so that the variable elements can be added to the other variable costs and the fixed elements can be added to other fixed costs.

In marginal costing, only the variable costs are charged to the units. The difference between sales revenue and the variable costs is not the profit, since no allowance has been made for the fixed costs incurred; it is the contribution towards fixed costs. Contribution is 'the additional profit that will be earned by an organization when the breakeven point production has been exceeded. The unit contribution is the difference between the selling price of a product and its marginal cost of production. This is based on the assumption that the marginal cost and the sales value will be constant' (Law, 2010, p. 110). Contribution can be calculated for one unit or for any chosen level of sales. The total contribution is the contribution per unit multiplied by the number of units produced. Contribution is important because once the total contribution exceeds the total fixed costs the business starts making a profit.

2. Explain the impact of limiting factors and how you would allow for them. Use a worked example to illustrate your answer.

A limiting factor is a constraint that restricts a business from achieving higher levels of profitability (for example a shortage of materials or labour, a restriction on the sales demand at a particular price or a limit in the production capacity of machinery). If the business has more than one product that uses the limited resource, it could mean that the business can only make a limited number of products and management needs to decide which products to make to obtain the maximum profit. The general rule is to maximise production of the product with the highest contribution per unit of limiting factor.

The example should show how the contribution per unit of limiting factor has been calculated and how selection will maximise overall profitability.

3. Villiers Engineering Ltd

The report should include the following points:

- The total cost per unit increases because some costs are fixed. Therefore, the same total amount of cost has to be shared over fewer units.
- Marginal costing focuses on the contribution to fixed costs. In periods of recession, most decision making is concerned with achieving the best contribution. Although in the long term it is essential that fixed costs are recovered, marginal costing can give a new perspective on the problems confronted by the businesses.

4. Paddington Ltd

(a)

Marginal cost statement 1 unit

	£
Revenue	10.00
Variable costs	
Direct materials	(1.00)
Direct labour	(5.00)
	(6.00)
Contribution	4.00

(b)

Marginal cost statement 12,000 units

	£
Revenue	120,000
Variable costs	
Direct materials	(12,000)
Direct labour	(60,000)
	(72,000)
Contribution	48,000
Fixed costs	(32,000)
Profit for the period	16,000

(c) The breakeven point is the 'level of production, sales volume, percentage of capacity, or sales revenue at which an organization makes neither a profit nor a loss' (Law, 2010, p. 65). At this point, total revenue equals total costs (or total contribution equals total fixed costs).

(d) Breakeven analysis

(i) BEP in units

$$\frac{\text{Fixed costs}}{\text{Contribution per unit}} \qquad \frac{£32,000}{£4} = 8,000 \text{ units}$$

(ii) BEP in sales revenue

BEP in units × Selling price   8,000 × £10   = £80,000

(iii) Sales activity to reach target profit

$$\frac{\text{Fixed costs} + \text{Target profit}}{\text{Contribution per unit}} \qquad \frac{£32,000 + £20,000}{£4} = 13,000 \text{ units}$$

(iv) Margin of safety

Selected level of activity – BEP in units   13,000 – 8,000   = 5,000 units

5. Soundtek Ltd

(a)

Marginal cost statement (1 unit)

	Standard	Superior	Deluxe
	£	£	£
Selling price	100	150	240
Variable costs			
Direct materials	(30)	(40)	(50)
Direct labour	(30)	(50)	(120)
Direct expenses	(10)	(25)	(24)
Contribution	30	35	46

(b) Contribution per £1 direct materials

	Standard	Superior	Deluxe
$\dfrac{\text{Contribution}}{\text{Direct materials}}$	$\dfrac{£30}{£30} = £1.00$	$\dfrac{£35}{£40} = £0.88$	$\dfrac{£46}{£50} = £0.92$
Ranking	1st	3rd	2nd

Interpretation: If direct materials are a limiting factor, maximise production of Standard, followed by Deluxe, and reduce production of Superior.

(c) Contribution per £1 direct labour

	Standard	Superior	Deluxe
$\dfrac{\text{Contribution}}{\text{Direct labour}}$	$\dfrac{£30}{£30} = £1.00$	$\dfrac{£35}{£50} = £0.70$	$\dfrac{£46}{£120} = £0.38$
Ranking	1st	2nd	3rd

Interpretation: If direct labour is a limiting factor, maximise production of Standard, followed by Superior, and reduce production of Deluxe.

(d) Other considerations (indicative)

- The analysis does not take into account that more than one of the two limiting factors identified may arise.

- Management may have overlooked other limiting factors (for example constraints on production capacity, constraints on sales capacity, obsolescence of its products through development of new technology).
- All the revenue and expenditure used in budgets are based on estimates and their utility depends on how realistic they are.
- Budgeted figures are only useful if there is frequent monitoring against actual figures and action taken to remedy any adverse variances.
- Budgeted figures may be difficult to predict for a new business or an existing business in a volatile market.

CHAPTER 7 BUDGETARY PLANNING AND CONTROL

1. Describe the main stages in budgetary control and the specific purposes of a system of budgetary control.

Budgetary control is the 'process by which financial control is exercised within an organization. Budgets for income and expenditure for each function of the organization are prepared in advance of an accounting period and are then compared with actual performance to establish any variances. Individual function managers are made responsible for the controllable costs within their budgets, and are expected to take remedial action if the adverse variances are regarded as excessive' (Law, 2010, p. 67).

The main stages in budgetary control are:

- Consult with managers to make assumptions and predictions about markets and business environment.
- Set financial objectives in the form of detailed budgets for income and expenditure for each function of the business.
- Once the budget period begins, continuously compare actual performance against the budget.
- Revise the budget or take remedial action to ensure financial objectives are achieved.

The overall purpose of budgetary control is to help managers plan and control the use of resources in a systematic and logical manner. This helps ensure that they achieve their financial objectives, which are:

- Profit satisficing (making a satisfactory level of profit).
- Profit maximisation (making the maximum profit).

The overall purpose of budgetary control is to help managers to plan and control the use of resources. However, there are a number of more specific purposes.

- A formal system of budgetary control enables an organisation to carry out its planning in a systematic and logical manner.
- Control can be achieved only by setting a plan of what is to be accomplished in a specified time period and managers regularly monitoring progress against the plan, taking corrective action where necessary.
- By setting plans, the activities of the various functions and departments can be co-ordinated. For example, the production manager can ensure that the correct quantity is manufactured to meet the requirements of the sales team, or the accountant can obtain sufficient funding to make adequate resources available to carry out the task, whether this is looking after children in care or running a railway network.
- A budgetary control system is a communication system that informs managers of the objectives of the organisation and the constraints under which it is operating. The regular monitoring of performance helps keep management informed of the progress of the organisation towards its objectives.
- By communicating detailed targets to individual managers, motivation is improved. Without a clear sense of direction, managers will become demotivated.
- By setting separate plans for individual departments and functions, managers are clear about their responsibilities. This allows them to make decisions within their budget responsibilities and avoids the need for every decision to be made at the top level.
- By comparing actual activity for a particular period of time with the original plan, managers can identify any variance (difference), expressed in financial terms. This enables them to assess their performance and decide what corrective action, if any, needs to be taken.
- By predicting future events, managers are encouraged to collect all the relevant information, analyse it and make decisions in good time.
- An organisation is made up of a number of individuals with their own ambitions and goals. The budgetary control process encourages consensus by modifying personal goals and integrating them with the overall objectives of the organisation. Managers can see how their personal aims fit into the overall context and how they might be achieved.

2. Discuss the advantages and disadvantages associated with systems of budgetary control.

The main advantages of budgetary control systems to cover in the discussion are:

- All the various functions and activities of the organisation are co-ordinated.
- Accounting information is provided to the managers responsible for income and expenditure budgets to allow them to conduct variance analysis.
- Capital and effort are used to achieve the financial objectives of the business.
- Managers are motivated through the use of clearly defined objectives and the monitoring of achievement.
- Planning ahead gives time to take corrective action, since decisions are based on the examination of future problems.
- Control is achieved if plans are reviewed regularly against performance.
- Authority for decisions is devolved to the individual managers.

The main disadvantages to cover in the discussion are:

- Managers may be constrained by the original budget and not take effective and sensible decisions when the circumstances warrant them. For example, they might make no attempt to spend less than maximum or make no attempt to exceed the target income.
- Time spent on setting and controlling budgets may deflect managers from their prime responsibilities of running the business.
- Plans may become unrealistic if fixed budgets are set and the activity level is not as planned. This can lead to poor control.
- Managers may become demotivated if budgets are imposed by top management without consultation or if fixed budgets cannot be achieved due to a lower level of activity beyond their control.

3. Explain the difference between a fixed budget and a flexible budget, using an example to illustrate your answer.

A fixed budget is 'a budget that does not take into account any circumstances resulting in the actual levels of activity achieved being different from those on which the original budget was based. Consequently, in a fixed budget the budget cost allowances for each cost item are not changed for the variable items' (Law, 2010, p. 193). It can be contrasted with a flexible budget, which is 'a budget that takes into account the fact that values for income and expenditure on some items will change with changing circumstances. Consequently, in a flexible budget the budget cost allowances for each variable cost item will change to allow for the actual levels of activity achieved' (Law, 2010, p. 195).

The example should show how a flexible budget changes in accordance with activity levels and reflects the different behaviours of fixed and variable costs.

4. MacDonald's Farm Ltd

Budget report for March			
	Budget	Actual	Variance
	£	£	£
Income			
Strawberries	25,000	24,500	(500) A
Blueberries	18,000	17,200	(800) A
Raspberries	19,000	19,600	600 F
	62,000	61,300	(700) A
Expenditure			
Salaries	28,400	29,000	(600) A
Expenses	12,500	12,000	500 F
Administration	1,800	1,700	100 F
Miscellaneous	700	300	400 F
	43,400	43,000	400 F
Profit for the period	18,600	18,300	(300) A

5. Green and Fair Ltd

The answer should be in the form of a report. A variety of approaches can be taken, but a useful method of analysis is to use the list of features that describe an effective system of budgetary control given in the chapter. Recommendations will depend on the assumptions made, but should be credible and set within a business context.

CHAPTER 8 STANDARD COSTING

1. Direct materials price variance

> = (Standard price − Actual price) × Actual quantity
> = (£4 − £3) × 5 kg
> = £5 F

Possible reasons are the use of inferior quality materials, a cheaper supplier or bulk discounts.

2. Direct materials usage variance

> = (Standard quantity − Actual quantity) × Standard price
> = (1,000 tonnes − 995 tonnes) × £50
> = £250 F

Possible reasons are the use of better quality materials with less wastage.

3. Direct materials price variance

> = (Standard price − Actual price) × Actual quantity
> = (£100 − £98) × 52 kg
> = £104 F

Direct materials usage variance

> = (Standard quantity − Actual quantity) × Standard price
> = (50 kilos − 52 kilos) × £100   *Note:* Standard quantity = 200 kg/4 units
> = (£200) A

Total direct materials cost variance

> = Price variance + Usage variance
> = £104 − £200   (favourable price variance but adverse usage variance)
> = (£96) A

Possible reasons are the use of inferior materials leading to higher wastage than planned, or the use of a new supplier who provides materials with a slightly different specification, leading to higher usage. Higher marks can be achieved for suggesting where the responsibility lies and for making recommendations for further action.

4. Speedy & Sons Ltd

Direct labour efficiency variance

= (Standard hours − Actual hours) × Standard rate per hour
= (500 hours − 460 hours) × £9
= £360 F

Direct labour rate variance

= (Standard rate per hour − Actual rate per hour) × Actual hours
= (£9 − £11) × 460 hours   Note: Actual rate = £5,060/460 hours
= (£920) adverse

Total direct labour variance

= Efficiency variance + Rate variance
= £360 − £920   (favourable efficiency variance but adverse rate variance)
= (£560) A

Possible reasons are that more highly skilled labour has been employed than planned and their output has been greater. Perhaps unplanned bonus payments have been made to encourage higher levels of productivity. The effect of these actions has led to an overall adverse variance of £560 and higher marks should be given for suggesting what possible actions can be taken to remedy the situation.

5. Accord Ltd

Calculated the direct material and direct labour variances and reconcile standard and actual costs.

	£		£	
Standard prime cost of actual production (7,500 × £80)			600,000	
Direct materials usage variance [(7,500 × 8) − 125,000] × £4	(260,000)	A		
Direct materials price variance (£4 × 125,000) − £252,000	248,000	F		
Direct labour efficiency variance [(7,500 × 6) − 91,000] × £8	(368,000)	A		
Direct labour rate variance (£8 × 91,000) − £313,500	414,500	F		
Prime cost variance			34,500	F
Actual prime cost of actual production			565,500	

INDEX